Remember

Norma A. Hawkins

ISBN 978-1-68517-285-5 (paperback)
ISBN 978-1-68517-659-4 (hardcover)
ISBN 978-1-68517-286-2 (digital)

Christian Faith Publishing, Inc.
832 Park Avenue
Meadville, PA 16335
www.christianfaithpublishing.com

Printed in the United States of America

Acknowledgments

To Sandy Birge, my niece

Oh! What a blessing you are, dear Sandy!
You've made my dream come true!
By typing, editing, and making calls
To tell me what I needed to do

Your skill, your patience, your attitude
Made everything fall into place!
My book will be published now I know
Made possible by you and God's grace!

My love and appreciation,
Aunt Nonnie
Norma A. Hawkins

Contents

Lyrical

Friends and Family

Holidays

Teacher and Her Students

Narrative

Thoughts

Introduction

(What is poetry? Let me try to describe it for you in a poem I wrote.)

Poetry is the way you feel
As you walk in the rain;
Fly in an airplane;
Drive in a new car;
Step in fresh tar.

Poetry is music that throbs
When the wind gently blows;
When a rooster crows;
Laughter ringing;
Warped doors swinging.

Poetry is all that you see
When you climb a mountain,
Or watch a fountain;
Stroll down a street,
See fields of wheat.

Poetry is the air you breathe
The pain and joy you hide
Way down deep inside;
Your secret thought,
A fight you've fought.

Poetry is the beat of your heart
That forces feeling through
Every part of you.
Now, do you see—
You are poetry!

Spiritual

I Met Him at the Altar

I met Him at the altar when I laid aside my sin,
And joyfully I praised Him as His love came surging in.
We left the church together, this newfound Friend and I,
His presence was so precious I felt like I could fly.

I lay down on my pillow, not a tear came to my eye,
For I knew I'd go to Heaven in the future by-and-by.
Our friendship grew more precious as the days and weeks rolled on,
I knew He was beside me, for He gave to me a song.

The first thing in the morning when I woke up from my rest,
I knelt down to my bedside and *oh*, how I was blessed.
The last thing in the evening, at the closing of the day,
I knelt once more to ask Him to guide me on my way.

One night I was so sleepy, I thought I wouldn't pray,
So, I asked God to forgive me. Thus, I blindly went astray.
One thing led to others, I forgot my blessed Guide,
And scarcely did I notice that He wasn't at my side.

It seemed I was so busy with my work and with my play,
That I found no time for worship, and had no time to pray.
For months I was indifferent until fear began to grow,
That if I should die a sinner, would I be prepared to go?

I knew that God was working and I knew that I was lost,
    'Til finally I decided that I would pay the cost.
    I met Him at the altar, and gave my life, my all
To that Never Failing Savior who will never let me fall.

This time I mean to serve Him and I'm going all the way,
    With Him along beside me, I can never go astray.
Oh, thank you, Lord, for warning me of the danger I was in,
    Thank you, blessed Jesus. Now I'm free from sin.

He Is

I hear God's voice in the gentle breeze
That lifts and caresses the twisting leaves,
He speaks to me, or so it seems,
In the murmuring babble of the rippling streams,
His voice I hear in the turtledove,
The tone, compassionate, soft with love,
I hear him speak in the roaring sea,
"Peace, be still," He says to me.

I feel God's touch in the gentle rain
That waters the earth and cools my brain,
I feel His touch in the sun's warm rays
That enfold me securely on summer days,
That touch is soft as the budding rose
Whose scent arises and pleases my nose,
I feel His touch when a snowflake drifts
Onto my hand, and my spirit lifts.

I see God in the mountains that rise
To the limitless space of dappled skies,
I see Him in a bird on the wing,
Who, in all situations, can only sing,
I see His love in a baby's eyes,
His compassion in the Christians' lives,
I see His Word as it lives and breathes,
In the acts of one who sincerely believes.

How do I know that God is real?
I see Him, I hear Him, and above all, I feel.

Music God Created

When God created the heavens and earth
He also included music and mirth.
Think of the millions of sounds that we hear,
God truly loves music. He's made that so clear.

Hear:
The wind whistling gently through autumn leaves,
Birds singing joyfully in all kinds of trees,
Brooks babbling laughingly over time-worn rocks,
Woodpeckers noisily tapping with determined knocks.

The waves of the oceans lapping the shores,
A baby mouse squeaking across kitchen floors,
A sassy squirrel scolding high on a limb,
A night owl hooting when daylight grows dim.

All of these and a million more sounds
Are witness to me that music abounds.
A true love of music our creator has shown,
For He has created all the sounds we have known.

Which sound is His favorite? Can you not guess?
It's the sound of music that He created to bless!
The song that comes from deep inside one
Who worships and praises God, Spirit, and Son.

Our worship to God is such a great treasure,
Remember the purpose is to give our Lord pleasure.
Maybe the sound isn't what we'd suggest,
But do the music and words pass the Lord's test?

Are we singing to please Him and not for ourselves?
Or are we allowing our voices to sit on the shelves?
Does our worship show honor and glory to Him,
Or are we allowing our worship and praises to dim?

No matter the talent, whether by note or by ear,
No matter what genre of the music we hear,
It will please the Lord wholly, not just in part
As long as the music comes straight from our heart.

A God-Given Responsibility

When you were given this little bundle of joy,
You'd be so happy with either a girl or a boy,
Did you realize then that parenting would be
Such an awesome, God-given responsibility?

Two little hands reaching out to you,
Two little eyes watching whatever you do,
Two little feet walking wherever you lead,
And a bright little mind to relate each need.

Loving your child is the easy part,
Nothing is sweeter than love from the heart.
God gives each parent a wonderful guide
That promises help when it is applied.

Train up your child in the way he should go,
Tell him about Jesus who loves us all so,
Read from the Word and teach him to pray,
So, as he grows older, he will follow Christ's way.

Your little child, so happy and whole
Has been given by God an eternal soul,
That is the challenge which all parents face,
To teach each child about His amazing Grace.

In Appreciation of Pastor Dennis Rogers

What can I say to a godly man
Who's been part of our lives many years?
A man who's become like our family,
Sharing our laughter and tears?

Thanks for your prayers on our behalf
When some rough times crept into our life,
Thanks for the help and support you gave,
Enabling our faith to survive.

When Jeff and Chris were still in their teens
You were their favorite youth pastor,
Remember that game you played in the park
That ended in such a disaster?

How well we remember one day in court
When your presence brought sweet peace of mind,
Remember when Mom lay sick and called you one night
And you were so gentle and kind.

When Jeff went to war in Desert Storm,
Cold fear saturated my soul,
In wisdom, you assured me he'd be fine;
He returned from Iraq safe and whole.

Through three cancer surgeries for Norm and me,
And Norm's heart surgery, too,
Your faith and prayers reminded us
That our God is faithful and true.

Remember our meals each Thursday night!
How we shared such fun altogether;
I always looked forward to those weekly meals
Regardless of inclement weather.

Life's ever changing, sometimes with no hint
Of what lies ahead for tomorrow,
Yet one fact remains forever the same,
God will be there in every tomorrow.

Happy Birthday

(To the pastor who married Norm and I in 1949. He has gone on to meet the Lord he served so faithfully.)

Happy birthday, Pastor Hyllberg,
May God grant you many years,
May He ever bless and keep you
From all heartaches and all tears.

May His spirit daily strengthen,
May His sunshine give a smile,
May His presence make you happy,
May He guide you all the while.

When He leads you through the waters,
And a storm begins to brew,
Look ahead and find the rainbow
That He's promised just for you.

When your trials sore depress you
And you just can't understand,
May you sing a song of gladness
As He firmly holds your hand.

Happy Birthday, Pastor Hyllberg,
And thanks for all you've done,
For you truly are a blessing
To us, each and every one.

Into the Desert

Into the desert the Spirit led
And I, not understanding why, said,
"Why the desert where hot, burning sand
Drifts in the air and covers the land?"

"Follow me, child, and be not afraid;
This is a trip I've already made,
I know it's a challenge, this barren place,
'Twas here I met Satan face-to-face."

"He'll come to tempt you as he did me,
But the power of the Word will set you free.
He'll try to tell you to praise *His* name,
Tell him your tired of his losing game."

"I will give you the right words to say,
Rebuke the tempter; He'll go away,
Then fall on your knees in prayer, and fast
Until your burdens are lifted at last.

"Rest in God's love and peace for a while,
You'll find the desert was not a trial
But a training camp for what I've planned,
And in this desert, you've learned to stand."

Out of the desert, the Spirit led,
And I, now understanding why, said,
"Thank you, Lord, for the dry barren place
That helped me grow in power and grace."

Questions

What in the world are you doing
To spread the gospel news?

Where in the world are you going
To share your Christian views?

When in the world will you follow
The pathways He will choose?

How in the world can you win souls
If you're not aware of their cues?

Why in the world do you wonder
That there are millions of empty pews?

Be a winner: Share Christ with a sinner!

A Shadow

I am sure that devil knows me,
By my first name and my last,
He surely knows how to trip me
As he chases me so fast.

How he loves my every weakness,
How he gloats when I forget
That I'm not to lose my temper,
And I'm bowed down with regret.

How he grins when I am sassy,
How he chuckles with delight,
When I make up some excuses
And stay home on my church night.

How he likes to whisper to me,
"You're too busy now to pray."
How his wicked eyes must brighten
When I insist on my own way.

Oh, yes, and he reminds me,
"Leave your Bible on the shelf,
There's so much you can be doing,
Take some time out for yourself."

But with Jesus as my Savior,
I have nothing now to fear,
And I'll live my life a Christian,
With my leader always near.

"So, Satan, you won't bother,
For I've Jesus as my guide,
And you'll never make me falter,
When I keep Him at my side."

Thoughts about Jesus

He's the one who loves me best
Even though He knows the worst about me.

The one who gives me a song
Even though He knows how often I cry.

He's the one who gives me yet another opportunity
Aware that I'll probably blow that one too.

The one who gives me hope
Even when darkness seems to overwhelm me.

The one who accepts me and understands all my idiosyncrasies
While others shake their heads and walk on.

The one who encourages me with "You can do it,"
When all others urge, "You might as well give up."

He's the one who listens compassionately
when a trial brings me low,
The one who holds all answers, He's the dearest Friend I know.

He's the one who said, "Verily, I am with you always, even unto the
Ends of the earth," knowing how easily I become lost.

He's the one who took my hell-bent soul
and cleansed it with His blood,
And promised me eternal life in Heaven just because He loves me.

A Sacrificial Gift

Is there anything I can do, dear Lord,
Anything—great or small?
I dedicate my life, my soul,
I give to you my all.

I'd go to a foreign land, dear Lord,
And share your precious Word.
I'd tell of your love and saving grace,
To those who've never heard.

I go to church most all the time,
I praise and worship you,
Isn't this sufficient, Lord?
What else is there to do?

What's that you're saying to me, Lord?
I hear your pleading voice.
You're telling me to do still more—
And in doing so—rejoice?

What is it, then, you ask of me?
Just show me; lead me to it.
Whatever it is I know that you
Will help me, Lord, to do it.

You're asking, do I love you, Lord?
Of course I do; you know it!
You say you have a perfect way,
Of helping me to show it?

You what? My money, Lord?
I pay my ten percent,
I give in special offerings, too,
Until my budget's bent.

A sacrificial gift, you say
Beyond what I have planned,
A gift that shows my love for you,
Yes, Lord, I understand.

What's mine is yours, I truly know,
I'll give as you've implored,
A sacrificial gift I'll bring
Because I love you, Lord.

Reactions and Reflections

Sunday we were thrust to the edge of hell where we witnessed Satan's powerful attempt to destroy us, and the battlefield was our own sanctuary. The following comments are based on the reactions and reflections of our church family when our church was bombed in Danville, Illinois.

The blast that rocked our building shook everything but our faith in God. The shock that ensued was stamped on every face. *Love* was personified in the tender hugs, the words of encouragement and the ministering to those who needed physical help.

Many of you expressed how strongly you sensed the presence of the Lord, from the moment of the blast and throughout those dreadful first hours. I, too, sensed His love and His concern for us, but I also sensed His fierce, protective shield over us, for what was perpetrated against us, was perpetrated against God.

After the initial shock abated, anger surfaced. Know this; our enemy is not a person or persons, but Satan himself, who compelled his pawn(s) to do this horrible thing. He has persecuted the church throughout the ages, but knowing his time is limited, his efforts are accelerated. Many of you said that we as a church are doing something significant enough for the furthering of the gospel, to warrant Satan's individual attention.

Now, determination has set in. Many of you are saying, "We're not going to let this keep us from worshipping the way we always do." Helen said, "When we go back in, I'll sit where I always sit!" (Which is in the damaged area.)

One common emotion that's threaded throughout everyone who was there Sunday is thankfulness; thankful there were no fatalities, thankful there are no life-threatening or permanent injuries among our casualties, thankful that we have a mature Christian body of believers to draw strength and support from during these stressful days. Most of all, we're thankful for the Word of God and His promise that He will never leave us nor forsake us.

Yes, reality has set in. It did happen—not just to our church but to other churches in the area and nation. But now is not the time to retreat in fear nor to waste time demanding why. Now is the time to put on the whole armor of God (Ephesians), stand up and be counted for the Lord, and know; "If God be for us, who can stand against us?"

Beyond the Bomb

On May 24th of 1998
We sat here at church about ten,
The ushers were standing across the front,
Ready for the collections to begin.

All of a sudden, without any warning,
A horrible blast hit the west wall,
Chairs were flying, and much debris
Was endangering and wounding us all.

Pastor stood and quietly spoke,
"Go quickly out the south door."
There was no screaming or shouting out,
Some were talking, but praying more.

God was there throughout this ordeal,
By His grace, we all were alive,
In spite of our enemy's attempt to destroy,
Our church has continued to thrive.

We grew closer and loved each other
More than we ever had before,
We learned through this terrible tragedy
That God is still watching o'er.

Let's not forget what the Lord has done,
Or what He has brought us through,
And though we're experiencing rough seas again,
Trust Him, and see what He'll do.

Remembering always how faithful God is,
Continue to pray and believe,
Live for Him daily and stay in his Word,
Then, His blessings we'll surely receive.

The Worth of Living

Above the mountains' swollen crest,
Beyond the shadows of the pine,
Still higher than the eagle's nest,
So wings this soul of mine.

Removed afar from living's chore
To dwell with timeless glee
Where obligations are no more
And routines cease to be.

A secret place that each must find
Known but unto God,
So delves the mystery of the mind
To tease you as you trod.

Resist the urge to be content,
For life is but a span,
Desire and habit leave a dent
Upon the souls of man.

Take flight above this present earth
And conquer worries, tasks, and fears.
Dwell with One who knows the worth
Of living, not of years.

A Prayer for My Friend

Lord, I come to you know on behalf of my friend,
His trials come at him with no visible end,
His spirit is low, he's bowed down with despair,
So, I bring him to you in sincere, earnest prayer.

Lord, help him feel your presence each day,
Encourage his heart to praise you and pray
In faith believing, that you'll answer his prayer,
May he know beyond a doubt that you are right there.

You see his heartache, his pain, and his grief,
Give him an anointing of blessed relief,
Remind him, dear Lord, that he is your own,
You have not forgotten him, he's never alone.

Lord, help him to lay his cares at your feet,
To trust in you wholly 'til his victory's complete,
Lift up his spirit, inspire him to praise
The redeemer who's loved him all of his days.

Remind him, dear Jesus, that during each trial,
You'll be there with him all of the while,
I'm asking, Lord, that he'll feel your sweet touch,
I know that to him, Lord, that will mean so much.

Thank you, Lord!
Amen

A Little Faith

A little faith in a great big God
Will mighty mountains move,
Faith as a grain of a tiny seed
Will his divine power prove.

A little faith in a great big God,
Yes, the size of a minute seed,
A grain of faith in His mighty name
Is all you really need.

The faith of a little child is all
That God requires of you,
He'll answer prayer and lift your care,
Where He finds such faith, He'll do.

A little faith in a great big God
Can accomplish impossible tasks,
Remember that faith as a little seed
Is all He ever asks.

What Be My Goal?

To work for power, gold, and fame?
To win a socially prominent name?
To have a crew at my command?
To tower o'er the lesser man?
Is this my goal?

To get what always I desire?
To someday set the world on fire?
To satisfy my greedy heart?
To ne'er do good on any's part?
Is this my goal?

To live expressly for myself?
To leave God's work upon the shelf?
To turn my ear from the warning bell?
To live and die and go to hell?
Is this my goal?

Or do I want to do what's good?
To understand and be understood?
To give my neighbor an honest smile?
To do only that which is worthwhile?
This is my goal.

To live for Christ a life anew,
To him be steadfast, sure, and true,
To witness to my fellow man,
To tell of Him the best I can,
This is my goal.

To live the Bible every day,
To work and watch and daily pray,
To go to Heaven when I die,
To live eternally on high,
This is my goal.

His Way Is Planned

You can't always see the things God has planned,
But He moves with compassion, His nail-scarred hand,
You may question or wonder or falter or doubt,
But God has already mapped the way out.

But you can't see the light when darkness surrounds,
Or hear the Master when Satan abounds,
You can't feel His presence when sorrows abide
If you fail to remember that it was for *you* he died.

You can know He loves you, if you trust in His word,
You can feel Him near when you call Him "My Lord!"
He does care and answer; We will give you the power
To conquer the sorrow and grief of this hour.

He'll never forsake you or leave you alone,
He still rules and reigns on His heavenly throne,
He still has the answer and He loves you and cares,
In spite of your heartaches, He'll answer your prayers.

Being a Witness

Do you know someone who is hurting?
Is there something that you can do
To ease the pain or frustration
Of this one God's assigned to you?

Are there people who don't know Jesus
Living or working nearby?
Have you been a living witness?
Are you willing today to try?

Jesus gave us all an assignment
Just before leaving this earth—
Go ye into the whole world
And share God's plan of new birth.

You don't need a passport or visa
Or a special call from the Lord,
He's recruited us all for such action
As he's instructed us in His Word.

He won't send us out all alone,
He's promised to be our true guide
The Holy Spirit will prompt us
To put our reluctance aside.

Does your heart yearn for the people
You meet in your world every day,
To lead them to Christ as their Savior
By the way you live and the words you say?

Maybe you don't feel the calling
To go to a faraway shore,
But you should feel the need to witness
To the neighbor who lives next door.

The challenge to be His witness
Is still just as urgent today
As it was when Jesus said it,
Just before His going away.

You're with Me

I don't understand the heartaches
That come along my way,
I don't understand the trials
Or the storms that cloud my day.

But I understand you love me
And you died for every sin,
So, give to me the *courage*, Lord,
To have sweet peace within.

I don't understand this journey
That you've led me on today,
But I understand You're with me
Every step along my way!

He Whispers

If we walk with God in the sunshine,
He will walk with us through the night.
If we pray to ask him for guidance,
He will keep our pathway alight.
Though we pass through the valley of sorrow,
He will never let go of our hand,
Though the mystery of death confounds us,
He whispers, "I understand."
Though the world is no longer a haven,
And our hearts bend low with despair,
Though the long, lonesome pathway grows weary,
He whispers, "I love you and care."

A Determined Woman

She'd wasted much time on many physicians,
But to tell you the truth, she grew worse,
She'd suffered through methods and medicines,
And she'd long since emptied her purse.

One day she heard someone calling, "Here's Jesus!
See miracles wherever he goes."
She knew in her heart this man could heal her,
If only she could just touch his clothes.

So, she joined the throng that followed the Savior,
Pressing closer and closer to Him,
The crowd was rough, and she had to be strong,
But her faith did not waver nor dim.

At last, she could reach Him; she fell to her knees,
Crawling forward among all of them
Trembling excitedly, because she had faith
To be healed when she touched His hem.

The Lord felt her touch and asked His disciples,
"Who touched my clothes?" They did not know.
The woman came, fell before Him, and said,
"I touched your hem; now I've been made whole."

He said to her, "Daughter thy faith made thee whole,
Go in peace and be cleansed evermore."
She rejoiced for she knew she was healthy,
And so much stronger than she'd been before.

We, like this woman, can receive from the Lord
Whatsoever our need is today,
Reach out and touch Him, in faith believing,
He will answer each time when you pray.

Daily Nourishment

With joy and peace, I am so blest
When in the rush, I stop to pray,
Prayer helps me stand the daily tests
That hover over every day.

The cares of life grow strangely dim,
And problems I have had to bear
I take in confidence to Him,
Oh, how sweet! My time of prayer.

I rise with hope and strength anew,
My faith in God restored once more,
He gives me strength that I might do
Things thought impossible before.

When I'm too pressed to take the time
To seek the Master's face each day,
Too soon I realize that I'm
The one to lose when I don't pray.

Somewhere, I've Lost Something

Somewhere, Lord,
Among the events of these
Last trying months and weeks,
I've lost
Something.
I should search for it
But I'm not sure
What it is
I'm looking for.
Your love, LORD?
No, I can feel your love
Enfold me
At every crisis moment
Your peace, Lord?
No, for in spite of
The wild leaping of my emotions
I sense a calmness,
A serenity
That I can't understand,
That I just accept
As a gift from
You, Lord.
Your guidance, Lord?
Perhaps.
I've reached
Too many crossroads
To have confidence
In my own ability

To make wise decisions—
But that's a positive,
Because now I find
I am compelled
To trust You
More than ever.
My friends, Lord?
Oh no, Lord!
My friends are
Walking by my side,
Hurting when I hurt,
Smiling when I can smile,
Urging me,
Encouraging me,
Inspiring my faith
To reach beyond
Today's heartaches.

So, what have I lost, Lord?

Ah, Now I see!
I've lost
The trivialities that clung to me
That fed my pride
And self sufficiency
That made me seek
No help from Thee.
Now they're missing.
Thank God, I'm free—
Free to depend
Entirely on Thee!

Jesus

He's the gentle rain
After a dry spell.
The healing touch,
When I'm not feeling well.
The cleansing force,
That took my sin.
The giver of peace
Down deep within.

He's
The Son of God
But an earthly friend,
Divine in nature
Who loves without end.
A blessed comfort
When I'm distressed
An encouragement
When I'm oppressed.

He's the one who walks
Close by my side.
Who gently and surely,
My steps will guide.
He dries my tears
When my heart is broken
And answers prayer
When my need is spoken.

He fills me with
The Holy Spirit
And speaks to me
When I will hear it.
He is the life
That dwells in me
And someday surely
His face I'll see.

Cleanse Us

God would have us
Pure and white,
Never wrinkled, but
Our garments bright.

Dear God, press us,
So, we may be
Righteous and holy,
Ready to meet thee.

Wash us and cleanse us
Under that flow
Of Calvary's slain lamb,
'Til we're whiter than snow.

Oh, Glory to God,
Forever we'll sing,
This song of redemption,
Our praises will ring.

Lyrical

(This section of poems is a group of songs I wrote but did not publish.)

That's When You Need Him

When the storm clouds gather 'round you
And winds of sorrow blow,
That's when you need Him,
When the tossing waves surround you
Raging to and fro,
That's when you need the One
Who did to Calvary go.

When a loved one has been taken
And you feel so all alone,
That's when you need him,
When your faith in God is shaken,
And your burden is unknown,
That's when you need the One
Who reigns on Heaven's throne.

When your last word has been spoken
And Death has called your name,
That when you need Him,
When your earthly ties are broken,
All fortune, wealth, and fame,
That's when you need the One
Who suffered for your shame.

That's when you need the One who died upon
A rugged cross to save
A weary, sin-sick world from judgement and the grave,
When your journey here is ended
And time shall be no more,
That's when you need the One
Who'll lead you to that shore.

He's Got a Miracle for You

Though your troubles seem like mountains
God can move them at His will,
Though life's stormy billows threaten,
He can tell them, "Peace, be still."
Though your sins may be as scarlet
He can wash them white as snow,
When Jesus saves a sinner, that's
The best miracle I know!

Though your life may be in shambles,
He can straighten out the way,
Though you cannot face tomorrow
He will keep you through today,
Though you feel there are no answers
To the problems plaguing you,
If you'll put your faith in Jesus
Your miracle He will do!

He's got a miracle for you
What you ask Him—He can do!
For there's nothing in this life
That God can't bring you through,
So, exercise your faith and pray
And believe Him when you say,
"He's got a miracle for *Me* today!"

When I Make It through to Heaven

When I make it through to Heaven,
It's because He holds my hand,
I don't have the strength to make it on my own,
When my heart is heavy-laden
I need God to take command
For at times I feel discouraged and alone.

When I make it through to Heaven,
It's because somebody cares,
And because of friends who help to bear my load,
When I cannot see an answer,
To my pleading, earnest prayers,
I need their help to keep me on the road.

When I make it through to Heaven
It's because of God's great love,
That sent His Son to suffer in my place,
When I reach those gates of glory,
Waiting for the saints above,
It's because of God's amazing, matchless grace.

Tell Me Again Today, Jesus

Tell me again today, Jesus,
That you love me as one of your own,
Though you've told me so many times, Jesus,
And so often in many ways shown,
How I love to feel the sweet joy,
As your love flows through my soul,
How I love to dwell in your presence
Once again to feel fresh and made whole.

Tell me again today, Jesus,
That you are concerned about me,
Let me listen again as you whisper,
"My child, I can hear your heart's plea."
Tell me again today, Jesus,
Just what you would have me to do,
Then give me the strength and the wisdom
To follow you all the way through.

Tell me again today, Jesus,
How much there is yet to be done,
And burden my heart for lost sinners,
That through me the lost can be won,
Tell me again today, Jesus,
"Have patience, I'll answer your prayer,"
Remind me I'm often too worried,
Remind me you'll always be there.

Remind me again today, Jesus,
How often I've failed you each day,
Remind me to follow more closely
Lest my life should lead one astray,
Tell me, again, today, Jesus,
That life on this earth is not long,
Tell me to trust you in all things,
And praise you each day with a song.

God Is a Game Some People Play

God is a game some people play
By going to church and pretending to pray,
By giving a one, a five, or a ten,
Depending on how entertaining it's been,
By singing hymn when the page is given,
By saying, "Oh, yes, I believe in a Heaven."
God is a game, a dangerous game, some people play.

God is a game some people play
When fortune and fame have come their way,
When life is so smoothly skimming along,
Everything is right and nothing goes wrong.
When friends and family show they care
Then—God is a game, a deadly game, some people play.

God is a game some people play
'Til suddenly on life's final day
They discover too late—God is living indeed,
And for His love and mercy they plead,
Realizing the truth—God is no game,
God is no game to be played—
God is God, an almighty name, to be prayed.

God is a game some people play
Trying to push all their guilt away
But God is no game—He is God!

Just Once More

Old Sampson had the power
To slay a thousand men,
The spirit was upon him
Time and time again.
Until he laid his head
In the lap of worldly sin
And knew not it had lifted—
No spirit of God within.

Old Sampson's eyes were blinded
His mighty locks were shaved,
And ridiculed by his captors,
He became a slave.
Until one day they led him
Into a public court
And bound between two pillars,
He cried, "Lord, once more."

Like Sampson in the Bible
I need a touch from you,
A portion of thy spirit
Will help me make it through
For every day I find, Lord,
As I walk toward Heaven's shore,
I need a fresh anointing
Just once more.
Just once more.

Just one more
Put you hand on me, Lord,
Just once more.
Let your spirit move within me,
Just once more.
Just once more.

Live in the Presence of God

There may be days when the sun
Seems to hide itself among
All the dark clouds that hang overhead
But his promises are true
He has not forsaken you
Just remember the things He has said.

When all the burdens you bear
Seem to be more than your share,
And the presence of God seems far away,
Ask yourself the reason why
You do not feel Him standing by
Oh, beware! It's so easy to stray.

Yes, it's the little things in life,
That can cause much pain and strife,
Satan tries to delude the souls of men,
He will catch you unaware
If you don't spend time in prayer,
Then you'll not feel God's presence again.

Live in the presence of God
Let His peace flood your soul,
Put Him first in our life every day.
Walk in the light of His word,
Give to Him full control
Live in the presence of God, all the way.

How Do You Do?

How do you do,
When your plans don't turn out right?
How do you do?
When the preacher's out of sight?
How do you do,
When your path is dark as night?
How do you do?
How do you do?

I'm feeling fine—
You answer those who want to hear
"I'm feeling fine—"
When really life for you is drear,
"I'm feeling fine—"
You answer smiling through the tears,
"I'm feeling fine.
I'm feeling fine!"

What do you know,
About the Christ who died for you?
What do you know,
About the act of praying through?
What do you know,
About a home beyond the blue?
What do you know?
What do you know?

I'm telling you,
There is a way out of your sin,
I'm telling you,
To ask the Savior to come in,
I'm telling you,
Your every battle He will win,
I'm telling you,
I'm telling you.

How do you do,
Well, I'm so glad you're doing fine!
What do you know!
Now you're a Christian friend of mine,
I'm telling you,
To let your light for Jesus shine,
How do you do—
You're doing fine!

Greater Is He

The rougher the pathway,
The closer He walks,
The fiercer the billows,
The calmer He talks,
The darker the shadows
And deeper my night,
The sweeter His presence,
The brighter His light.

The harder the trials
I meet day by day,
The tighter His handclasp
That shows me the way,
The bigger my heartaches,
Or the storm clouds above,
The weaker my courage,
The stronger His love.

For greater is He that lives in my heart
Than he would tempt me from God to depart,
The greater the battle, the greater the prize,
And I'm looking forward to a home in the skies.

It's Time to Go Home

It's time to go home—I can see every sign
That the prophets of old, said we surely would find,
I look at the clouds, and expect them to part,
It's time to go home, I'm yearning at heart.

It's time to go home, my treasures are there,
And nothing in life here on earth can compare,
To the blessings of God and the beauty we'll see,
It's time to go home, can't be too soon for me!

It's time to go home, sinner listen to me,
Unless you repent, too late it will be,
God sees your distress, and He covets your soul,
It's time to go home; won't you give Him control?

It's time, it's time, it's time to go home,
I'm tired of this world with its heartache and its grief,
It's time, it's time, it's time to go home,
I'm homesick for Heaven, and I'm ready to leave.

There'll Be Somebody Waiting for Me

When I've shed my last teardrop
And I've climbed my last hill,
When I've fought my last battle,
And my heartbeat grows still,
When I've come to the banks
Of the Old Jordan's tide,
There'll be somebody waiting
On the other side.

When I've finished my journey
Through life's rugged storm
And my ship's found a harbor
Where it's sheltered from harm
When I've cast down my anchor
And I'll need it no more,
I know Jesus is waiting
On the other shore.

Somebody's waiting
With arms opened wide,
Waiting to greet me,
On the heavenly side,
I've no fear of tomorrow,
Or of death facing me,
There'll be Somebody waiting,
Yes, waiting for me.

Touch Me Today

Lord, forgive my unbelief,
Bring to me to a sweet relief,
You have promised you would heal,
Now your mighty power reveal.
Lord, you've said, "Where two or three
Are gathered, there I'll surely be."
Lord, now I plead; answer my need; and touch me today.

Lord, you've promised in your word,
That before we speak, you've heard,
You can know my needs today
Though my heart's too full to pray,
Just the power of your name
Can heal the deaf, the blind, the lame,
Touch me, Oh Lord; as in your word; touch me today.

I want to feel your hand on me,
I want to hear you call my name,
I want to know you've set me free
And I'll never be the same;
I need a healing touch from you,
I need to know your word is true,
Touch me, I pray; in your special way; touch me today.

Look Who's Coming!

It is written in the Bible
That the Savior shall return
There are signs of His appearing
If we know them, we can learn,
And according to the scriptures,
It can't be long, I know,
'Til my Jesus shall come back,
Then, Praise God! I'm gonna go.

The dead in Christ shall quicken
In a twinkling of the eyes,
Then we alive, remaining,
Will join them in the skies,
There's no time for preparation,
There will be no time to pray,
Now's the day of your salvation,
Look who's coming—any day.

I'm so glad I took my Jesus
As my Savior, guide and friend,
And no matter how soon He's coming
I am ready for the end.
I've no fear of His returning,
As I daily watch and pray,
Lift up your heads, oh Christians,
Look who's coming any day.

My God Will Provide

I've no need to feel lonely or worried inside,
For has God not promised that He will provide?
I never will doubt him when sorrows abide
For my God has promised and my God will provide.

I have peace and contentment I never could hide
For what I am needing my God will provide.
Whatever the conflicts or troubles be tide
I lean on His promise and my God will provide.

My God will provide what I need for each day
He walks by my side as He shows me His way
He will not permit that my prayers be denied
For all of my victories my God will provide.

But in the Meantime

I've heard about that city fair,
With walls of precious stone,
I long to see the mansions there
God is building for His own.

I want to leave this world of care
And enter Heaven's door,
I long to meet my Savior there
And praise Him evermore…

In the meantime, until He comes again,
I'm gonna tell the world my Lord will save from sin,
I'm gonna labor until the trumpet beckons me.
And though I'm longing to enter Heaven's gate,
For Heaven's glories, I'm gonna have to wait,
But in the meantime, I'll lead the lost to Calvary.

Is It Not Written

Burdens so heavy you can't walk along,
Doubts make you question, is God on the throne?
Then comes the answer, God's promise is true,
Is it not written that He'll take you through?

When you are laden with trouble and woe,
When all around you, life's stormy gales blow.
Search in the scripture, rejoice in God's word,
Is it not written and has He not heard?

Is your heart heavy and endless the night?
Does it seem often that nothing goes right?
Whisper a prayer and He'll give you a song,
Is it not written to Him you belong?

Is it not written, He cares for you?
That which He's promised, surely He'll do.
Is it not written, He'll lift your cares?
Has he not promised to answer your prayers?

Seek the Will of Jesus

Seek the will of Jesus before you do
Anything that people might ask of you,
Go into your closet and pray, pray, pray,
Until He clearly answers, "My child, this is the way."
Only in the center of His will can you find,
Meaning, joy and happiness and blessed peace of mind,
He saved you for a purpose, you're part of His plan,
So, seek the will of Jesus and not the ways of man.

Worldly men may tempt you with offers of gold,
They say to enjoy life before you grow old,
They think fame and fortune each man should pursue,
But the only place of blessing is in God's will for you.
See the will of Jesus when setting your goal,
Nothing can you profit should you lose your soul,
Tell Him you are willing to do His command,
Then seek the will of Jesus and not the ways of man.

Let Your Joy Bubble Over

If your face is much too long,
Then there's surely something wrong,
Where's the joy of your salvation that you claim?
If you find it hard to smile
When you're going through a trial,
Then smile a victory in Jesus's name.

If to sinners you look blue,
As though God's forsaken you,
They will say, "Well, we don't need a dose of that!"
For it's only with a grin
You will draw the sinners in
Let the sunshine of your smile show where it's at!

Try not looking so abused,
Act a little more enthused,
You will find that people notice something real.
Make the world a better place,
Let your joy shine on your face,
It's surprising how much better you will feel.

Let your joy in the Lord bubble over,
Let it brighten everything you do;
There's a sad world outside,
So don't you try to hide
The joy that the Lord has given you.

Is Anybody Up There?

One day when I was feeling low in spirit,
My faith in God was growing very dim,
He tried to speak, but I didn't want to hear it,
I was too busy blaming things on Him.

I cried, "Oh, Lord! Is anybody up there?
Do you really listen when I pray?
Sometimes I feel my prayers are getting nowhere,
Come down, oh Lord, and sweep my doubts away."

Not many days had passed 'til something happened,
I knew that God alone could intervene,
I called on Him and Praise the Lord, He stepped in,
How things can change when God is on the scene!

I shouted, "Lord! I know you're really up there,
And I know you really hear me when I pray,
For now I know my prayers are getting somewhere,
You came, oh Lord, and swept my doubts away."

I Don't Want Anything to Keep Me From Reaching Heaven Someday

If my daily walk's not close enough
And my life's a stumbling stone,
Just remind me, Lord, of Calvary,
And the cross you bore alone.
And if people watching day by day
Can't guess I am your own,
Then by your spirit, speak to me,
Until I kneel before Thy throne.

If the things of earth should tempt me
Such as power, wealth, or fame,
If I'm selfish in the way I live
And I feel no guilt or shame,
If my life becomes so taken up,
My Christian walk grow lame,
Then by your spirit, deal with me,
Until I call upon your name.

I don't want anything to keep me
From reaching Heaven someday,
For there is nothing in this world
That makes me want to stay,
I know that Jesus is my Savior,
He will help me day by day,
I don't want anything to keep me
From the straight and narrow way.

Later

Had my life all planned ahead,
Really meant it when I said,
Gonna have my share of fun,
Won't depend on anyone.
I pursued my plan with zeal,
Life, to me, was one Big Deal,
Each success that came along
Assured me nothing could go wrong.

When God's spirit spoke to me
Saying, "Child, I'll set you free."
"Free from what?" I said, "I'm fine!
I control this life of mine.
I'm only doing what I choose—
With my luck, how can I lose?
Holy Spirit, go away,
Come back later, not today."

Then one day, my pain began
Failure came into my plan.
All I'd gained had disappeared,
Nothing left but what I feared.
Life had played a trick on me,
I'm no longer young or free,
I can't make it on my own,
I can't stand to be alone.

Then God's Spirit spoke to me,
Saying, "Child, I'll set you free,"
"Please," I cried, "I need you so;
Lord, don't ever let me go.
I said "later" once before,
Enter now through my heart's door.
How much grief I've borne by choice
By saying 'later' to your voice."

Look Ahead

Look ahead, look ahead,
Where is your pathway leading?
Look ahead, look ahead,
Is the road rough and steep?
Look ahead, look ahead,
Is it trouble you're breeding?
Look ahead, look ahead,
Wake up from your sleep.

Look around, look around,
Where is your destination?
Look around, look around,
Is the way dark and drear?
Look around, look around,
Have you made preparation?
Look around, look around,
Will you face death with fear?

Look inside, look inside,
Is it right with your maker?
Look inside, look inside,
Do you know how to pray?
Look inside, look inside,
Can you see your Creator?
Look inside, look inside,
Let Him have His own way.

Look ahead, look around,
Look inside, my dear brother,
Don't delay, don't delay
Give Him your all in all,
He'll forgive, He'll forgive,
Such a friend, you've no other,
Oh, what peace, oh, what joy,
When you get down and pray.

Look above, look above,
There can be no deceiving,
Look above, look above,
And you must be sincere,
Look above, look above,
All it takes is believing,
Look above, look above,
You will find Jesus near.

Look ahead, look ahead,
And before it's too late,
Turn around and go back
Where you know Jesus waits,
He will lead you on safely
To that far golden shore,
So, turn back, yes, turn back,
And go straying no more.

You Need Faith

If your life is filled with fear and disillusion,
Everything seems fake and nothing's real,
All the treasures you seek are but illusions,
Nothing can describe the way you feel.

Look around, you will find no satisfaction,
No joy, no peace of mind anywhere,
The world seeks to tempt you with attractions,
Telling you it's fun and games out there.

Then you need faith to give your life direction,
And you need faith to rest your weary soul,
Accept by faith the cross and the resurrection,
And through faith, you'll be redeemed and whole.

My God Will Provide

I've no need to feel lonely
Or worried inside,
For my God has promised
That He will provide.
I never will doubt Him
When sorrows abide,
For my God has promised
And He will provide.

I have peace and contentment
I never could hide,
For what I am needing
My God will provide;
Whatever the conflicts
Or troubles betide,
I lean on His promise
And God will provide.

My God will provide
What I need for each day,
He walks by my side
As He shows me His way,
He will not permit that
My prayers be denied
For all of my victories
My God will provide.

I Wouldn't Want to Go Anywhere without Him

I've been in the valley of gloom and despair,
But walking beside me, my Jesus was there,
Oh, I wouldn't want to go—Anywhere without Him;
I've wandered in darkness, sorrow and grief,
One touch of His hand gave me blessed relief,
Oh, I wouldn't want to go—Anywhere without Him.
In all life's situations, I'm glad to know He's mine;
For when Jesus walks beside me, I can go anywhere, anytime.

I've been on the mountain of glorious height,
Jesus was present to share my delight,
Oh, I wouldn't want to go—Anywhere without Him;
I've traveled the pathway of comfort and ease,
Still, he was with me, sharing His peace,
Oh, I wouldn't want to go—Anywhere without Him.
In all life's situations, I'm glad to know He's mine;
For when Jesus walks beside me, I can go anywhere, anytime.

I've stood at the corner, not knowing which way
Would lead me to victory, 'til Jesus did say,
"Oh, you wouldn't want to be—Anywhere without Me."
Then, choosing the pathway, He told me to choose,
I know in His will that I never would lose,
Oh, I wouldn't want to go—Anywhere without Him.
In all life's situations, I'm glad to know He's mine;
For when Jesus walks beside me, I can go anywhere, anytime.
He died on the cross to give me new birth
And yes, though I journey the ends of the earth,
Oh, I wouldn't want to go—Anywhere without Him.

I'm Invited
To a Royal Coronation

I've never been invited to the White House,
As far as they're concerned, I don't exist
For my name will never be among the famous,
But I'm glad I've been included on God's list.

I'm related to no wealthy dignitaries,
Unimportant seems to be my family name,
But in the Book of Life my name is written,
To God's royal family, I've got a claim.

I have been to many splendid celebrations,
But I've never met a king or president,
Now I'm going to a royal coronation,
I am going to take part in that event.

I'm invited to a royal coronation
When they crown Him King of kings some glorious day
Christians will be there from every tribe and nation,
I'm so excited, I've been invited, on that day!

He Will Always Hold Your Hand

No matter how high the mountains
You must climb along the way
No matter how dry the desert
You must wander through for days,
No matter how deep the rivers
You must cross to higher land,
No matter where He leads you,
He will always hold your hand.

No matter how hard the trials,
You must bear from day to day,
No matter how many teardrops
Seem to flow when you pray,
No matter how big your burdens
Or impossible your plans,
For no matter where He leads you,
He will always hold your hand.

He will always hold your hand,
If you stay close by his side;
He will lead you through to safety
If you'll let Him be your guide,
Don't try to make the journey
From this earth to heaven's land,
Unless He's there to help you
'Cause He'll always hold your hand.

Eternity Will Tell

Why do little children suffer
And the blind not see?
Why do wicked people prosper
The guilty go free?
Why must those who call on Jesus
Suffer agony?
We'll never know while here below,
But eternity will tell.

Though we let our lives be guided
By his mighty hand,
Still, we carry many burdens
We don't understand;
We forget the blessed Savior
Has complete command,
But God does care, He's still up there,
And eternity will tell.

Why should Jesus choose to save me
From my sin and shame?
Why, when I didn't know Him,
Did He call my name?
Why should He love and forgive me
When I finally came,
I cannot say until that day,
When eternity will tell.

Yes, eternity will reveal life's hidden secrets,
All the answers to our questions, doubts, and fears,
And eternity will unveil that our God can never fail,
He was walking close beside us, down through the years.

Yes, I Will Trust in the Lord

Though my youth has forsaken me
Troubles o'ertaken me
Yet, I will trust in the Lord.
Though the storms blow around me
And problems confound me,
Still, I will trust in the Lord.

What a wonderful life it's been
Walking each mile with Him
Yes, I will trust in the Lord.
And no matter what lies ahead,
I will not fear nor dread,
Because I will trust in the Lord.

He has proven His love for me
Dying on Calvary,
Yes, I will trust in the Lord.
When I've needed Him—night or day,
He's never far away,
Yes, I will trust in the Lord.

Through so many dangers I've already come
He's brought me out safely through everyone,
I'll believe in Him, cling to Him,
Praises I'll sing to Him,
Yes, I will trust in the Lord.

There Goes a Child of God

I may not measure up to this world's standards
Or have a social rank or wealth or fame,
But one thing I confess
That when I've done my best
Someone will say of me,
"There goes a child of God."

My name will never be engraved in statues,
I'll prob'ly never see the world at large,
But, Lord, one thing I ask,
When I've done my final task,
Someone will say of me,
"There goes a child of God."

No streets will bear my name nor books my history
No one will quote my words, nor sing my deeds,
But I will count it gain,
Though unknown I remain,
If men can say of me,
"There goes a child of God."

There goes a child of God
I hear the way he talks
I see the way he walks
And the life that he lives,
There goes a child of God,
I feel the prayer he prays,
It shows in a hundred ways,
The goes a child of God.

Tomorrow on My Mind

Many people in this world
Seem to live from day to day,
Never caring that tomorrow
Things of earth shall pass away.
Pleasure is a way of life,
To eternal things they're blind,
All their fears, they hide,
Casting God aside,
There's no tomorrow on their mind.

Though I covet my todays,
God has been so good to me.
Still, I know that some tomorrow
I shall face eternity.
Life on earth is just a place
To prepare for life divine
While I watch and wait
I'll anticipate,
I've got tomorrow on my mind.

I've got tomorrow on my mind
For today will soon be past;
Tomorrow may be the day
When my Lord will come at last.
There's a longing in my soul
For the happiness I'll find
When Christ shall say, "You're home to stay,"
I've got tomorrow on my mind.

Praise the Lord; It Won't Be Long!

It may be that today He will call us away
From the midst of earth's turmoil and strife,
Oh, what glory awaits through those heavenly gates,
Yes, I'm longing for eternal life.

If your heart's full of sin, won't you ask Jesus in?
For tomorrow it could be too late.
When He calls for His own, you'll be left here alone,
So, accept Him today. Please don't wait!

Praise the Lord! It won't be long!
Hallelujah! What a song
We shall sing as we arise
To meet the Savior in the skies.
Oh! He'll meet us at the door,
Shouting, "Welcome evermore!"
Praise God! Praise God! It won't be long!

Headlines

You say you haven't noticed?
Then, brother, won't you look!
The headlines are fulfilling
What's written in God's book.
I read of many earthquakes
And wars across the sea;
Although the news is headlines
It's Bible prophecy.

The headlines tell of thousands
Whose hearts have failed in fear;
I cannot help but wonder–
Will he find faith down here?

Like men in times of Noah
So, we've become today;
The headlines surely warn us
He's coming any day.

Jesus is coming, the headlines tell me so,
Jesus is coming, it's almost time to go;
I read in the papers every single day,
That Jesus is coming and we all need to pray.

This Is the Hour

This is the hour,
Tomorrow is too late,
This is the hour,
He's standing at the gate,
This is the hour,
To prove his power,
We must be sure,
Our hearts are pure,
This is the hour.

The Lord is coming
Time swiftly passes by,
Will all be ready?
Will you let sinners die?
This is the hour
To prove His power,
We've work to do
Ere day is through
This is the hour.

The night is stealing,
Twilight is fading dim,
We've but a moment,
To win the lost to Him.
This is the hour
To prove His power,
Oh! Don't delay
Get down and pray
This is the hour.

Do you feel burdened
For those you dearly love,
Who when the Lord comes,
Will not be called above?
This is the hour
To prove his power
Beseech the Lord,
Believe His Word
This is the hour.

Your Redemption Draweth Nigh

There's a time that's coming very soon,
And it may be morning, night, or noon,
Then to things of earth we'll say goodbye,
So look up, for your redemption draweth nigh.

These are days that test our faith in God,
So stay in the narrow path He trod,
Never falter, never Christ deny,
But look up, for your redemption draweth nigh.

When you feel discouraged, and alone,
Just remember God is on the throne,
Satan to defeat you oft will try,
Then look up, for your redemption draweth nigh.

When He comes to catch His waiting bride,
To be ever with Him by His side,
We'll be glad we held His banner high,
And looked up for our redemption draweth nigh.

Your redemption draweth nigh,
Will you be ready?
Your redemption draweth nigh,
Will you be saved?
When He calls the saints away
You will have no time to pray,
Your redemption draweth night,
Oh! Don't delay.

When I Get Alone with God

When I get alone with God, I can feel His love for me,
I cry, and tell Him all that's on my mind,
Then as the teardrops fall, I hear Him gently say,
"I know the world is cruel, but, child, be kind."

When I get alone with God, His compassion floods my soul,
And before I've said a word, He knows my needs,
How I praise His Holy Name, I can never be the same,
When I've been alone with God, my soul He feeds.

When I get alone with God
I can feel my heavy burdens fall away,
When I talk to Him in prayer,
I know He hears me there,
When I get alone with God every day.

The Lord Is on His Way

Yes, the Lord is on His way,
He could come just any day,
And I want to make the rapture, this I know,
Yes, the Lord is coming soon,
He'll rise above the sun and moon,
And we'll sing and shout hosannas as we go.

You have got to be prepared,
If your mortal soul is spared,
From the wrath which lies ahead for those who're lost,
Yes, the Lord is on His way,
Seek Him now without delay,
'Cause to miss the rapture is not worth the cost.

There has never been a day
Just exactly like today,
Our battle's nearly won,
There has never been an hour
When we've felt His might power,
And the miracles being done.
There has never been a time
When I've felt as close as I'm
Feeling close to Him today,
There's a feeling in the air,
You can feel it everywhere,
'Cause the Lord is on His way.

Outside of Jesus

There's no joy in this life. Outside of Jesus,
There's no peace to be found in this place,
There's no chance of eternal salvation
There's no mercy, no pardon, no grace.

There's no love like God's love, Outside of Jesus,
There's no cure for the trials we bear,
There's no rest for the weary-worn trav'ler,
There's no comfort, and no one to care.

There's no shelter from storms, Outside of Jesus,
There's no faith in the future of man,
There's no way to escape from the Judgement,
There's no Calvary and no redemption plan.

Outside of Jesus, outside of Jesus
Outside of Jesus, outside of Jesus,
There's no hope of tomorrow,
Only death, pain and sorrow,
No sins are forgiven
And there's no hope of heaven.
Outside of Jesus, outside of Jesus
Outside of Jesus, outside of Jesus.

Where Are We Going from Here

This world's in an awful mess,
And so few seem to know
How to escape the distress
To whom or where they should.

The Bible is our true guide
It clearly points the way,
It's up to you to decide,
Where are you going today?

In spite of growing alarms
The future's in God's hand
Find safety within His arms
Give your life to His command.

There's a popular way of life
That seemeth right to man,
But death is the end thereof,
So why not follow God's plan?

Oh, where are we going from here?
Where are we going from here?
Heed my invitation to read Revelation
It tells where we're going from here.

Friends and Family

To My Sons

Often,
With bated breath
I've watched you step
Hesitatingly
Among fragile decisions,
Longing
To speak a word
Or stretch forth a helping hand
When you weakened.
But knowing
You wouldn't interpret
My interference
As love,
I silently prayed
That God would do what
I couldn't.
Proudly,
I've watched you grow and mature.
Humbly, I thank God for the men
You've become.

Love,
Mom

To Norm on Our Fiftieth

Norm, you and I grew up together,
We've walked hand in hand in all kinds of weather,
God must have used a permanent glue
To cement us together—me and you.

Sure, we've had words, sometimes loud,
Sure, we're both stubborn and somewhat proud,
Yes, there are times when we disagree,
But we love each other, Yesssssireeee.

Remember the years we worked so hard;
You operated a crane in the GM yard;
I taught school at Westville Jr. High,
My, how swiftly those years flew by!

Remember when Jeff was seriously ill?
But our God healed him. It was his will.
Remember when Chris had a heart attack,
And when we all prayed, God gave him back.

Remember last summer in Roanoke, VA
When I was afraid God would take you away?
But again, God answered our fervent prayer,
You're the picture of health, just standing there.

Remember the day of the awful church blast
When we wondered if that day would be our last?
And twice last year when I faced the knife,
We knew that our God had control of my life.

Remember the good times, the blessings untold,
Two wonderful sons, smart, handsome, and bold,
Two daughters-in-law we love as our own,
And six grandchildren, how quickly they've grown.

Remember the years when we traveled a lot
With a gospel group called "The Family of God"?
Ah, yes, Norman, those were the days,
God has blessed us abundantly in so many ways.

But now we look forward to what lies ahead,
And as we grow older, we will not dread,
For we know that God will be our guide
As the three of us walk, side by side.

Reminiscing from now to way back then
Prompts me to say, "Norm, I'd marry you again"!

Norm died January 12, 2009, two months before our sixtieth anniversary.

My Son, the Soldier

(Written while Jeff was fighting in Desert Storm.)

I watched my son when he was small,
He played for countless hours then
With army tanks and army trucks
And green plastic army men.

Military was on his mind,
Of that, there never was a doubt,
When he was asked what he would be,
"A US soldier," he would shout.

He went to Kemper as a teen,
A military school, you see,
The three years he attended there
Proved to us what he would be.

We watched him master every task
That military people do
And, proud of each accomplishment,
We marveled, yet somehow knew

That someday Jeff might have to go
Where wars are fought and blood is spilled,
Today we face reality,
US troops are being killed.

Today we bow our heads in prayer
As those we love tread burning sands
Not knowing what awaits them there
Beyond the sea in foreign lands.

Today, O God, I ask you please
Protect my son and all the rest
Who fight for freedom overseas,
Keep them safe, keep them blessed.

Send angels forth to keep a guard
O'er allied forces everywhere
And let all POWs know
They are daily in our prayer.

On Jeff's Return from Korea

(Jeff is retired as lieutenant colonel from the US Army and was European project director at Fort Eustus, Virginia.)

I'm so glad to have you home again,
This year has finally passed,
So often I have prayed for you
And now you're back at last.

I'm proud that you're a soldier
Who defends our native land,
I'm proud that you're a captain,
But most proud that you're a man.

When you were just a tiny babe
I thought I couldn't love you more,
But each day and year that passes by
Engenders more love than before.

When doctors said you'd surely die
Because your heart was bad,
I asked God to let you live,
He healed you. I was and am so glad.

But greater joy than this I felt,
When you prayed on bended knee
And asked the Lord into your heart,
That meant all the world to me.

Although tomorrow can't be seen,
Our god will make a way,
All He asks of us, my son,
Is to trust Him day by day.

A Prayer for Chris

Dear Lord, today this is my prayer:
Whenever Chris sits in this chair,
Of your sweet presence he'll be aware.

From the burdens give him rest
Each time he labors at this desk,
Reaffirm to him how much he's blest.

Ease his hurried, his worried mind,
Accented by his daily grind,
May in this room Your peace he find.

Guide each decision he must make
Prepare him to do what it may take
To be a blessing for his family's sake.
And he is!

If I Had a Daughter

(Two of the best daughters anyone could have, thanks to my sons!)

If I had a daughter
I'd want her to wear
Snappy bright eyes
And dark, shining hair.
I'd want her to walk
With a spring in her step
And have lots of energy,
Motivation and pep;
To be interested in people
And help when they hurt,
To be ready and willing
To play or to work…
If I had a daughter…
But, in a way, I do,
And strangely enough,
Now I have two, Brenda and Terri.

To Scott (Joy's Husband)

This is a tribute to a grandson of mine
Who goes by the name of Scott Emerine.
He's proven to us just what he can do
By graduating today from ORU.

This hasn't been a soft breeze for Scott,
He's had to work and achieve a lot,
Because in the middle of his college life,
He met a young lady who now is his wife.

They married, you see, while at ORU
And prayed for the Lord to help them through,
God led them off in a new direction
And promised them guidance and His protection.

They arrived in Virginia with praise in their mouth
That Jesus had led them to their family down south,
Scott found a job and a nice place to stay,
While meeting new challenges each stressful day.

He then made arrangements to complete his degree,
And finish he did, as you folks here can see,
During this time, quite a tough job he had,
In addition to which, Scott became a proud dad.

But he never gave up on his goal to achieve
A bachelor's degree that he now will receive.
We're proud of you, Scott; you're quite the man!
We know you'll continue to follow God's plan.

Whatever the future holds up ahead,
Remember the words that Jesus has said,
He'll be with you always, no matter what,
May you ever have happiness and sweet Joy, Scott.

A Gift of Love for Jan

A little red car that looks so happy
Has been repaired by your grandpappy,
He's very proud of that little car,
And, as its owner, we're sure you are.

We know you look with anticipation
For something nice for graduation,
So, we have a plan, Grandpa and I,
A plan we hope won't make you cry...

"We're going to pay," your Grandpa hollers
"The entire seven hundred and fifty dollars!"
The cost of fixing your little red Ford
Is our gift to you from us and the Lord!

Tyler Dale

You, Tyler Dale, have been born one year,
How quickly those twelve months have passed,
Every day you learn and you grow,
And you seem to do it so fast.

You are a bundle of energy
That keeps everyone on his toes,
You are a ray of sunshine and joy
That sparkles wherever he goes.

You are the answer to earnest prayers
A promise from God up above,
You are a gift to all of us,
Oh, how easy you are to love.

To My Brother Bob Tellier after His Tragic Accident

(Written to Bob in 1957 while he was in the Northwestern University Hospital in Evanston, Illinois.)

I tried to find a funny card
To make you want to smile,
But couldn't find a single one
That seemed to be worthwhile.

So, I'd like to try one of my own
To put in with my letter,
It will all be worth the effort
If it makes you feel some better.

My memory isn't very good,
But I can sure recall
A lot of things that have happened
To our family, one and all.

Remember when Mom and Dad were gone
And we played blind man's bluff,
And then we'd make a batch of fudge,
Then, man, how we would stuff!

Remember how we used to slide
Down the hill in a rusty tub?
And when we fell off to the side
We'd just get up and rub.

Though we didn't live in a mansion
Or a palace on a hill,
All the fun and laughter of the years
I can remember still.

Each year I'll cherish always,
As the best year of my life,
Including the happiness and joys
And the heartaches and the strife.

On Barb Tellier's Fortieth Birthday

Ronnie said the other day,
"I'm going to trade my wife away,
Now she's forty, I'll get two twenties,
I tell you, boys, I'll have fun a plenty."

But Barb replied, her patience tired,
"For two twenties, dear, you are not wired.
Besides, forty years isn't so long,
The older the fiddle, the sweeter the song."

Falling apart at forty, they say,
You're over the hill and out of the way.
But I'm here to declare to everyone
That going downhill can be lots of fun.

So, hang in there, girl, and don't regret,
There's a lot of good years left in you yet,
When you think of the choice you've had,
Growing old is not really bad!

To Allan and Marge

My, how the years so swiftly pass by,
And the older I get, the faster they go.
But it's hard to believe that Allan and Marge
Were married fifty long years ago.

They were so young when they began dating
They were not even dry behind the ears,
Yet, here we are today all celebrating
Their marriage of fifty years.

But from the very first day of their married life,
They seemed so happy together,
They made quite a pair—this man and his wife,
In the pleasant or the stormy weather.

I remember a winter that was so cold
But they never made a fuss
When they ran out of heating oil, we told
Them to come on and stay with us.

We lived together about three months
And what wonderful times we had,
Marge babysat and cooked our meals.
She and Al never got grouchy or mad.

They were such a joy to be around,
I was sorry to see them leave,
They went back to the house they'd found,
I'm sure, to them, it was a relief.

Allan's best friend, back in those days,
Was a man by the name of Red Green,
Those two guys had some humorous ways,
But sometimes their tricks were quite mean.

Now Bill, who's a cousin to this Red Green,
Is scared to death of any snake,
So, Al and Red put one in his mailbox,
Boy! What a racket did Bill make!

Margie stayed busy raising two girls,
And never had time to be lazy,
She seldom had time to sit down and rest
Except to play the piano like crazy.

For five years they were in a gospel group,
The Family of God singers were they,
Who traveled all over the Midwest states,
To cut records, minister and pray.

Al and Ron both built new houses
On either side of our mother and dad,
You'd better believe, their lives were changed,
What wonderful years they had.

Then Allan wanted to move way down here (Florida),
But Marge really did not agree
It was a time of frustration and fear,
But they finally moved down, you can see.

I'll never forget one October day
When Allan was with us one year,
I came in from the doctor who'd just had to say,
"You have breast cancer, my dear."

He could tell, I'm sure, by the look on my face
That something was certainly wrong,
He held his arms out and I fell in that place
Of his two loving arms so strong.

Sandy and Sue, you are so blessed
To have parents like God has given,
And all of your family need to make plans today
To meet them someday in Heaven.

To Marge and Allan, I love you so much,
You've been such a blessing to me,
May God grant you both many more years,
And many more anniversaries.

To Allan from Sis

For several years during the summer,
Allan stayed with Norman and me,
To work on construction in Illinois
The pay was better, you see.

What fun we had while he was here,
And what all he helped us do.
He helped us build a patio,
And a brand-new kitchen too.

He never complained about the meals
That a lousy cook served each day.
He was always in a pleasant mood,
No matter what came his way.

Until one Sunday, Al was so sick,
That to church, he did not go.
When we came home with food for him,
He said a definite, "No."

Ron and Norm took him to ER
Where the doctor met us.
"This man has appendicitis.
We'll operate, if he'll let us."

So immediately on that Sunday night,
The doctor operated.
Al said, "Call Marge when it's over."
And we all prayed while we waited.

God spared his life, that doctor said,
His appendix had already burst,
And peritonitis had set in.
The results could have been worse.

Allan's loved the Lord so many years
And served Him wherever he trod,
For five of those years, in many states,
He sang with the "Family of God."

Now he will sing without getting tired,
And without any worry or care.
Now, he's part of the real Family of God,
He is happy and blessed up there.

A Cruising Family Event

My brother, Larry, and his wife, Anne,
Can accomplish things that no one can.
They called our family with startling news,
"We're taking you all on a Bahama cruise!"
Oh, what joy! Oh, what bliss!
To be together on a trip like this!

The gospel concerts were such a delight,
And we watched karaoke 'most every night.
Our Dan entertained with a song or two,
The crowd really like him, I'm telling you.

Sharing memories of days gone by
Was so enjoyable, whether truth or lie!
Laughing, eating, and even while walking,
It seemed as though we were constantly talking.

Larry and Anne, we will never forget
The time spent together was the best time yet.
Hopefully, again in the days still ahead
We can meet once more, or in Heaven instead.

Thank God for the time and money you shared
To show all of us just how much you cared
That we needed time to spend with each other,
We children of such a fruitful father and mother.

As time goes by and years have passed
And we've all made it HOME at last,
We'll be so happy to see each other
And Norman, Bob, Al, Dad, and Mother,
But while on earth, we'll forever enthuse
About this family's Bahama Cruise.

(My youngest brother Dwight died in November 2019.)

To Stanley and Kay Hawkins on Their Fiftieth

On the nineteenth of December in '48,
Stanley and Kay could hardly wait
To begin their life of wedded bliss
As they promised, "I do," and shared a kiss.

God smiled on them because He knew
That Stanley and Kay would always be true
In spite of the trials that would come their way,
God knew their love was there to stay.

In about two years, Susan Kay was born,
A beautiful doll in lace adorned,
Then came Barry and how happy they were,
He'd carry their name and their lineage insure.

Just when they thought their family complete,
Along came Brian and he was so sweet!
Life became busier than ever before,
Good times and bad times came in at the door.

Each child's wedding and each grandchild's birth,
For Stan and Kay, had immeasurable worth.
They love each of you deeply and thank God each day
For the blessings He's given, and for all of you pray.

Love held them together down through the years,
Through miles of smiles and buckets of tears.
Not once, however, did they feel bereft,
For the Lord was beside them and He never left.

Fifty years later, Stanley and Kay understand
That the years of their lives are safe in His hand,
Whatever the future, they can face it with joy,
And with faith in their Lord that this world can't destroy.

Wm. Stanley Hawkins

Stan was a man who walked with the Lord,
Every step along life's way.
He followed the precepts of God's Word.,
He knew how to live, how to pray.

Stan loved his family so very much,
How proud he was of each one,
He nurtured them, provided for them
Through hard time and, yes, through the fun.

Stan drew friends like a giant magnet,
He was just that kind of man,
Always, it seemed, he was reaching out
To anyone who needed a hand.

Stan loved to share his sense of humor
With those who took time to hear,
Nurses at Sager loved his stories
About times and people so dear.

Stan trusted God with his life and his death,
His faith was steadfast and sure,
And though we'll miss him so much, we know
That same God will help us endure.

If Stan could talk to those left behind,
He'd say that life's trials—big or small—
Are naught in the light of eternity,
And heaven is well worth it all.

To Susan Kay on Her Graduation

How happy I was on a cold winter day
When a baby was born and named Susan Kay.
I felt that I was passing my prime
For you made me aunt for the very first time.

I remember your eyes and your heart-reaching smile,
I remember you learned in a very short while
To walk and to talk and to do funny things,
Like falling off counters and sliding out of swings.

You started to school and time went so fast,
From grade to grade you continually passed.
Then quicker than I could wink my left eye,
My little niece had started to senior high.

And now today, there's a lump in my throat,
For the day which I once thought so remote
Is upon us and you are graduated,
To me, you're a child, but time hasn't waited.

I've watched you mature in body, soul, and mind,
You've grown to be pretty, Christ-liked, and kind,
You've an inner strength that glows about you,
A faith that enables no one to doubt you.

Whatever God wills in the future for you,
Be humble and willing and eager to do.
For nothing surpasses the blessings He gives
To him who will follow, and in His will lives.

To Susan and John on Their Wedding Day

Two lives walked separately along a road
Through sunshine and the rain,
Searching, searching for a mate
To share the losses and the gain.

One day while walking, John met Sue,
(They smiled and talked of many things.)
Then John said softly, "I love you,"
And Sue replied, "My heart sings."

"Let's walk together," John said to her,
"And share what're may be.
I'll love, protect, and comfort you
And always treat you tenderly."

"Yes," she said, with smiling eyes,
"I'll walk with you along this road.
For I would welcome a helping hand,
To share my awkward load."

"I will love you as you love me,
With a heart that's ever true.
I give myself unto your care.
Yes, I'll walk with you."

And so they pledged their vows in June
Before their friends and God,
Now they're walking side by side,
Where countless couples trod.

Down the road that's full of snares,
With but their love to guide them,
But one bright promise, God has given,
He will walk beside them.

To Ed Tellier

Ed was a very kind, gentle man
Who could make you laugh, if anyone can,
He was such a pleasure to be around,
You never heard him put others down.

He loved to fish out in Kickapoo Park,
And to hunt mushrooms from dawn to dark.
He worked with wood like a talented pro,
And tended his garden to make things grow.

He loved to camp and ride in his boat,
And always he talked with a happy note.
He loved his kids, his grandkids, and life,
But most of all, he loved his sweet wife.

They fit together like peas in a pod—
Paula, his wife, and Ed and his God.
For he had accepted Christ years ago,
And served Him well daily, this we all know.

Today we surrender Ed to God's care
Knowing that someday, we can see him up there
In a place called Heaven, near God's throne,
If we, too, accept the Lord as our own.

Today may I say to all gathered here
In spite of our heartache, our loss, our tears,
If we love the Lord, we'll see Ed again,
When will that be? God alone knows when.

Grandma and Grandpa Richardson on Their Golden Anniversary

Two hearts can meet and fall in love
And make their vows to God above
To live together through all the years
Through sickness, sorrows, joys, and tears.

But time will find their love grown cold,
It isn't long until—Behold!
They're looking for a different mate,
So, seems to be the trend of late.

How glad the heart of God must be
When there's a couple He can see,
Who has lived together fifty years,
Despite those sicknesses, sorrows, and tears.

This pair was married in 1905,
And how that marriage has seemed to thrive,
They still walk together along the way
And keep the vows made on that day.

They started a home not far from here
With happy hearts that held no fear
Of what the years might hold in store,
For love to them meant forevermore.

And then it wasn't long, you see,
Until they started a family,
Bill and John then little Grace,
All decked out in frills and lace.

Then Doc and Edith, Woody and Gus,
And next, of course, came all of us.
And each little girl and each little boy
Has been to them a special joy.

How their family thanks God above
For giving them to us to love,
For moms and dads like them are rare,
And a lovelier couple there is nowhere.

Today our hearts all breathe this prayer,
"God Bless and keep this beloved pair
And grant to them many more years,
Many more blessings and many less tears."

Grandma, and you, Granddad,
We're thankful for the love you've had
That led to a wedding day of olden,
That today you celebrate as golden.

In Memory of My Grandparents
(Chris and Rachel Richardson)

I'd love to sit and talk with you
About so many things,
The years we shared together and
The joy that loving brings.

I'd tell you all about my kids,
How proud of them you'd be,
I'd love to hear you say again
How proud you were of me!

I'd love to listen to your tales
Of days long since gone by,
And marvel at your souvenirs
That made you laugh and cry.

I'd love to come and visit you
And sit around your table,
I'd love to lick the candy pan
And drink from the old, tin ladle.

I'd love to run across your yard,
And down through the garden gate,
I'd love to help you weed and hoe
From early morn 'til late.

I'd love to feel your gentle hug
That let me know you cared,
And hear the laughter in your voice
At something we had shared.

But most of all I wish that I
Could somehow let you know
That as the years pass swiftly by
I still love and miss you so.

To My Grandmother Rachel Richardson

She walked through life, in hand with God,
She walked by faith alone,
And now she walks where angels trod,
Around the heavenly throne.

She passed through earth with cheerful smile,
She sowed a blessed seed,
She passed through life with busy hands,
Helping those in need.

She passed through earth, yes, from our sight,
But never from our heart.
And someday in that city bright,
We'll meet no more to part.

God called her name and took her hand,
She followed Him in peace.
He led her to the Promised Land,
Where joys will never cease.

To Aunt Dorothy Richardson

(Loan manager at the bank.)

She was a lady, as everyone knows,
From the top of her head to the tip of her toes,
She walked through this life with strong, quiet step,
She made not a promise that couldn't be kept.

Friends were all drawn by her bright, winning smile,
And she always was willing to visit awhile.
Clients admired her business acumen,
And her integrity was quite superhuman.

Always, whenever we've needed a loan,
She did all she could, leaving no unturned stone.
To assure that our needs were sufficiently met,
She's helped so many people recover from debt.

Since moving to Heaven, her account is now changed,
She's been sending up deposits, her rewards are arranged.
She won't have to worry about war and strife,
She's enjoying the splendor of her eternal life.

To Uncle Gus Richardson

We have a special guest today with us,
He's a man I've always called "Uncle Gus."
He was born in September of twenty-two,
That makes him older than many of you.

Respect our elders we've always been told,
That's one advantage of growing old.
But Unc has never seemed old to me,
He's so young at heart and forever will be.

When he was just a boy in his teens,
He went into town and joined the Marines.
We all remember how he went to the war
And fought for our freedom on the enemy's shore.

When he returned, he found him a wife,
Who to this day, is the love of his life.
In the next several years, the children came,
Gayle and David, Susie and Jane.

He worked in construction many long years,
He overcame hardships with blood, sweat, and tears.
He finally retired from that daily grind
And left town for Florida, some pleasure to find.

Whenever he came back to visit awhile,
"Let's meet for breakfast," he'd say with a smile.
For he was determined to keep family united,
And in our company, he was really delighted.

Living in Florida, he had time to do
The small, tinkering things he wanted to,
But he missed his family and friends up here,
So he moved back to Danville, his hometown so dear.

Unc, you are known as a generous man
Who has often extended your strong helping hand,
To those who were hurting or just feeling low,
And you certainly did not do it to put on a show.

You'd be surprised, Unc, if I told you, indeed
How many people have watched you helping those in need,
Don't ever change, you have just the right touch,
We love and admire and respect you so much.

Your Niece, the one who made you Uncle or Grandpa, you asked.

To Uncle Bill Richardson's Eightieth Birthday

In the year of our Lord, in 1907,
A son was born to Rachel and Chris.
To them, Bill was a gift from Heaven,
Who grew in stature, from that day to this.

He lived on a farm during most of his youth
With four brothers and Edith and Grace.
He was famous for telling "mostly" the truth
And for fixing old clunkers to race.

Then he met Effie, who lived not too far,
And he knew he'd found him a wife.
Soon there were married and hitched to a star,
They lived together the rest of her life.

They had a daughter and two fine sons,
Patricia, Bill Jr., and Jim.
Five grandchildren and two great ones,
Yes, God's been so good to him.

He's shared God's love and saving grace
With every person he's met.
And when you see him, there's a smile on his face,
And a word of cheer, you can bet.

Because he did what all Christians should do
And witnessed each day of his life,
Most of our family is born again, too,
Thanks to Uncle Bill and his wife.

But that's not the end of the story today,
His feet with the gospel are shod.
He's living a life we can look to and say,
Indeed, there's a true man of God.

Betty and Burnell's Fortieth Anniversary

Let's take a walk down memory lane
With the Steelman's of yesteryears.
You see, we lived next door to them
And shared much laughter and some tears.

I remember well when Keith was small
And he hid from his mom and dad
Everyone in the neighborhood
Searched everywhere for that lad.

Then, when everyone had given up
And Betty said, "Let's call the cops."
Out from behind the big armchair
That sneaky little Keith pops!

One day a large swarm of honeybees
Flew in through my living room door,
I called Burnell who came running to help,
And swatted twenty or more.

I remember well when Joyce was born,
A month or so before her date,
I helped put Betty in the car
Then went home to pray and wait.

Then Jeff was born and Betty and I
Enjoyed our babies together.
Once, while they napped, we were talking
'Bout gardens, kids, and weather

When a Greyhound bus veered off the road,
"Come quickly," a rider plead,
"Our Greyhound bus is off the road,
I'm sure the driver is dead."

One evening, just about suppertime,
We heard a loud, thunder-like roll,
What a shock when we ran outside,
Steelman's house was in a hole!

The man who was digging their basement
Hit a support with his tractor,
The walls and floors were badly torn,
The future couldn't look blacker.

"Now where will we live?" the Steelman's cried,
"For certainly can't stay here."
So, they moved into our garage,
Until cold weather drew near.

Some months passed. They had moved down the road,
Betty called, her voice filled with fright,
"Something's wrong. I'm in pain," she said.
"And Burnell's working tonight."

"Hang on! We'll be there at once," I said
And quickly we pulled up outside,
Then off to the hospital we drove her
Oh, what a terrible ride!

The doctor came and gave us the news
"We have to operate right now."
"I'll go get her husband," Norm said,
"We'll be back in time, somehow."

Somehow, they were, and Betty survived
That night of unbearable pain.
God was there, and He takes good care
Of all who pray in his name.

Oh listen, my friends, those were the days.
Some were good, and, yes, some were bad,
But thanks to Betty and Burnell
Those were the best years we've had.

To Betty Steelman's Eightieth Birthday

John and Grace Richardson were all aglow,
They had a new baby, one you all know.

It was July 19th, nineteen twenty-three
When Betty was added to the family tree.

It's been a long time, but I remember still
How Mom and I would drive up Anderson Hill

To pick up Betty on most Friday nights
To babysit me and my brothers—"The Frights"!

Betty attended school at Catlin High,
"I'd sure like to visit," one day said I.

So, she took me to class, but I must have been bored,
Because I went to sleep and started to snore.

Poor Betty, I'm sure, was embarrassed to tears,
And I haven't forgotten, after all these years.

Upon graduation in forty-two,
Betty worked very hard at Musebeck Shoes.

About that time, I'm happy to tell,
She met a young man whose name was Burnell.

These two fell like a ton of red bricks
They were married February 3rd in forty-six.

This marriage was truly ordained in Heaven,
And Judy was born in July, forty-seven.

Life was exciting, life was just fine,
Then Keith was born in forty-nine.

What happened next was a blessing, you see,
For the Steelman's had moved next door to me.

Joyce came along in May, fifty-two
Two months later Jeff joined our crew.

Kenny was born in September, fifty-five,
Just nine days after my son Chris had arrived.

Connie was born in July, fifty-seven,
She was the last of Betty's bundles from Heaven.

Many things happened, both funny and sad,
But, oh, what wonderful moments we had.

Sometimes we'd pack up each girl and boy,
And go look for mushrooms. Oh, what joy!

When problems came (and we had our share)
Betty and I joined together in prayer.

Betty was always a fabulous cook,
On the making of pies, she should write her own book.

She worked very hard and helped those in need,
She was never too busy to do a good deed.

Betty loved God and lived in His word,
From the time they were babes, her family heard

How Jesus loves them and answers their prayers,
If they take to Jesus all their burdens and cares.

Her faith was the source of her life and breath
When in ninety-five, Burnell met his death.

She never wavered nor doubted the Lord
Knowing she'll see him someday, this man she adored.

Today we're so happy to celebrate
The birthday of Betty at this party, but WAIT!

Betty, hear us all say, "You're such a sweet lady,
And you do not look or act like you are now eighty!

Evelyn

Evelyn was born into this world,
The daughter of John and Grace,
With a zeal for life and a family to love her,
And a beautiful smile on her face.

Into her family also were born
Sam, Oliver, Betty Ellen,
Don't forget George and Sally Anne,
Imagine the action and yellin',

Evelyn attended Diamond School
Where the hearts of her teachers she won,
She made good grades and many friends,
And graduated in '31.

She wanted to go to Oakwood High
But her health would not permit it,
Instead, she learned by experience,
Wherever she could get it.

And learn, she did, so many things,
Like sewing, crocheting and cooking,
And all the while the boys observed
She certainly was good looking.

A certain young man from Iowa,
(Melvin Dodson was his name)
Arrived to visit in '35,
Evelyn's life was never the same.

When he returned to where he lived,
Young Melvin took Evelyn, too;
They married and settled in Iowa
And to each other were true.

Two children were born to bless their lives,
Larry and sweet Betty Rae,
They taught their kids to work with skill,
To love, to respect, and to pray.

In time, their children married
And grandchildren came—galore!
To Betty and Bob, God gave three,
To Larry and Ingrid, four.

But suddenly in '62,
Melvin passed away
So, Evelyn returned to Illinois
And decided that here she'd stay.

All of us—her family and friends,
Are glad she followed God's plan,
Not only did she bless our lives,
But God gave to her a man.

Bill Alpers was a Christian man
With qualities rare and fine,
So, Evelyn married Bill one day
In November of '69.

Their families blended into one,
Both sides had much to give,
The love, respect, and happiness
They shared will always live.

The years flew by; great-grandkids came
To bless their lives still more,
God's peace and joy surrounded them
In spite of some sorrows they bore.

Then in July of '85,
Bill heard God call his name,
He went to meet his blessed Lord,
While Evelyn had to remain.

Alone again, yet not alone,
For Jesus is always there,
She walks in faith through all her days
And breathes a constant prayer.

Some of us who live today
Are healthy and have succeeded
Because God answered her requests,
When Evelyn interceded.

Dedicated to Family of God Singers

Thirty years ago, God called us out
As soldiers to battle, we had no doubt
Going forth, we sang place to place
Songs about Jesus. His love and His grace.

Hearts were touched and so were we
As we traveled and sang about Calvary.
The battles raged on, savage and heated
But people were saved and Satan defeated.

Then twenty-five years ago, we disbanded.
Our separate lives to Him we handed
No longer a group but His soldiers still,
Each working and serving and doing God's will.

Then the Lord said, "I need you once more
Go forth and minister on Florida's shore
I know you are wounded and tired of the fight
You've fought many battles both day and night."

"But I will go with you, the battle is yours,
I'll lift up the weary and open closed doors,
So, once more to the front, though wounded and older
I promise to help you, just lean on my shoulder."

Dear Lord,
We're here again as soldiers for Thee
Use us, anoint us so others will be
Drawn to the cross and to you, our soon-coming King,
Bless us all now as we talk and sing.
Amen.

To Mike and Linda

We've known for some time that today would come
When we'd have to say our goodbye,
But that doesn't make it much easier
We'll probably all have a good cry.

May God go with you and use both of you
To witness to those you will meet,
May good health and happiness always abide
As you walk down your sun-filled street.

But please don't forget your friends here up north
Who dwell in this cold prairie land,
Invite us all down to visit sometime
And we too will walk in the sand.

Five years we traveled "The Family of God,"
And truly we were so blessed
We had lots of fun, and God gave us souls,
As we sang to the sad and distressed.

Mike, how I'll miss your playing guitar
Up on that platform each week,
Linda, your singing those beautiful songs
Lifted us all to a higher peak.

You're leaving a gap that cannot be filled,
But we know in God's master plan,
He'll send us someone to help with the work,
God has just the woman and man.

If wishes could make all our dreams come true,
You two would remain with us still,
But we understand and His ways are not ours,
So how can we question his will?

Bill and Elsie—Forty Years

Bill and Elsie grew up close,
With just a street between
They never dreamed that they'd become
Mr. and Mrs. Green.

But one day something happened,
A spark had kindled a flame,
Bill and Elsie fell in love,
They've never been the same.

On August the 30th
Of '47
A wedding took place
That was blessed in Heaven.

Bill and Elsie worked at a plant
Where the company made gloves,
They moved into a house nearby
And lived in peace and love.

One day, Uncle Sam called Bill,
And told him, "We want you."
So Bill then joined the Air Force
And flew off into the blue.

Well, really, they flew to Idaho,
A place called Mountain Home.
Where life became quite hectic
(But that's not the end of my poem.)

Someone told them of Jesus
And they called upon His name,
Bill and Elsie's life together
Has never been the same.

But as the years were passing by,
One dream was unfulfilled,
They hadn't any children,
And how many tears were spilled.

Then one night at the altar,
The people gathered round,
They prayed for Bill and Elsie
And the power of God came down.

Then miracles of miracles
In 1961
God heard their prayers and answered.
Bill and Elsie had a son.

These dear people were so blessed
With friends from everywhere,
They're quick to tell the people
How Jesus answered prayer.

A Tribute to Bill and Elsie

We're going to miss you, Elsie and Bill,
You're leaving a big pair of shoes to fill,
For thirty-some years you worshipped with us,
And did many things, such as driving the bus,

Or teaching a class, and playing guitar
Working for Jesus, how faithful you are!
We do understand why you're moving away
But that doesn't erase our heartache today,

We remember the years we sang as a group
What great times we had! My, what a troop!
We remember the times when the going was tough,
You never stopped praying—you called Satan's bluff,

You've helped many people who needed a hand,
Sharing a love that's your own special brand,
You never expected or wanted our praise
For the countless good works that filled up your days.

You've served God so faithfully for so many years,
And though we will miss you, we say through our tears
May God's richest blessings continue to fall
When you're living in Florida, having a ball.

We're going to miss you, that much I know,
Because, my dear friends we do love you so.

Carolyn Haas Tribute

I've known Carolyn almost all of her life
As a beautiful person, mother and wife.

A wonderful hostess who time and again
Opened her home to all who dropped in.

There was always such fun, such chaos, and mess,
How she remained so calm is anyone's guess.

Her laugh was infectious, her smile, warm and sweet,
The friendliest woman you ever could meet.

Respected in town as a skilled beautician,
Considered by some to be part magician.

Loved by her grandchildren, you can be sure
By the notes they have written especially for her.

People who knew her thought it not odd
That she traveled and sang with the Family of God.

For music brought Carolyn much joy and delight,
Her alto voice helped our choir sound just right.

But consider this thought that will surely inspire,
Today Carolyn's singing in a heavenly choir.

To Minnie Haas

The greatest treasure that man can behold
Lies not in the sparkle of diamonds or gold—
Or yet in the charisma of power or fame—
Or in the strength of a world-famous name.

But oh, how priceless a life that's lived well
That inspires us with feelings our tongues cannot tell.
We admire and respect when so rarely we find
A person like Minnie, she's one of a kind.

Down through the years so freely she's done
Whatever was needed to make the church run,
Teaching our children with true dedication—
Holding meetings in jail for many years' duration.

Conducting church downstairs every Sunday
So, our children will grow as Christian's one day.
Attending all services and never complaining
If the preaching is long, or if it is raining.

Though we can't begin to repay what we owe her—
By our actions today we're trying to show her—
"Minnie, we love you, for all you have given—
Your rewards will o'er flow someday in heaven."

Carl Hettsmanberger on His Eightieth

I've known Carl for many long years,
In fact, he even had hair.
I lived next door while he dated Margaret—
They were such a romantic pair.

They married and Carl went off to the Army
While Margaret stayed home and cried,
But finally, one day Carl DID return,
They began their life side by side.

When Jim was born, how proud they were
Of their beautiful brown-eyed boy,
In about two years, son Gary was born
To add more depth to their joy.

Then Gayle was born! A girl at last!
Their pride just simply exploded,
Their dream came true and even more joy,
And their home was completely loaded.

By far the most significant event
That happened in Carl's life,
Was the night he invited the Savior in,
Both he and his beautiful wife.

They served the Lord so faithfully,
They raised their children in church,
To find a couple more dedicated than they,
You'd really have to search.

During these years we were their friends,
And, oh, the fun we all had,
Boating, swimming, learning to ski—
Our lives were so happy and glad.

One day while boating, a storm blew up,
We hurried to reach the shore,
But we had to anchor under the bridge
And watch the storm billow and pour.

Carl's boat, a Larson, with outboard motor,
Was such a beautiful blue,
But once while riding, his motor cover
Wobbled and then off it flew.

He dived and dived, to no avail,
That cover was gone for good,
But he didn't get mad, he kept his cool,
Just like a good Christian should.

Carl was our Sunday School Superintendent,
The leader of quite a team,
And every year on the Fourth of July,
It was his job to get the ice cream.

He always enjoyed those little kids
Who lined up for their treat,
Their screaming and yelling, he didn't mind,
Even when they stepped on his feet.

The years elapsed, and the kids were married,
Then God called Margaret's name,
Carl's life, I know, from that day forward,
Has never been the same.

More years passed by and we lost touch,
I don't know about this part of his life,
But I know Carl has always served the Lord,
Through the good times and the strife.

We're glad to have Carl here with us today,
Still serving the Lord of his youth,
His positive works and his attitude
Are a blessing to all. That's the truth!

He and Mary make such a good team,
They visit the sick and the old ones,
I know when the crowns of life are bestowed,
Theirs will both be gold ones.

So, Happy Birthday, Carl, my friend,
May the Lord give you so many more,
But regardless of the time we do or don't have,
We'll meet on that beautiful shore.

Ramona

Some people are teachers
To be seen of men,
Some try to tickle the ears.
But you are a teacher
Who knows where we've been,
Who shares in our laughter and tears.

We've all watched your life
In good times and bad,
We're proud of your faith that shines out.
You've lived by example
The lessons we've had,
You've shown how to trust and not doubt.

We hope that our presence
Will somehow convey
How we love and appreciate you.
May God's richest blessings
Surround you each day
In all you so willingly do.

Iota's Homegoing

Can we bestow
A smile to show
How much we truly care?
Is there some way
For us to say
She was so sweet, so rare?

She's spent her life
As mom and wife
And servant to her Lord,
Throughout the years
Her smiles and tears
Have been a silver cord.

A cord that binds
The Hearts and minds,
Of those whose lives she touched
And so we say
On this, her day,
We love you, oh, so much.

For every year
She was given here
We thank the Lord above
Happy Going Home
Know this, Iota, you're loved!

To Mary on Her Ninetieth Birthday

Ninety years ago
God sighed and said,
"I need a special friend."
And so, he created Mary:
Knowing she would be true to him.
All her life,
God decided to give her
A long, fruitful one.
And sure enough!
She's walked with Him
Through valleys and mountains,
Laughter and tears,
Grief and joy,
Pain and peace.
Steadfast, loving her Lord
More each passing year.
Her children, watching her example,
Marvel how she gives so much of herself,
To them and others
And still has so much left
To share again and again.
But Mary can,
Because she's God's special friend.

Will the Real Man of the Year Stand Up?

Is there a man in this world today
Who always puts other folks first?
Who cares for the old, the sick, the poor,
And serves those who hunger, who thirst?

Is there a man in this world's mess
Who refuses to dwell on the can'ts?
Who overcomes daily the negatives
And ignores the ravings and rants?

Is there among us anywhere
Or in any other state
A man who conducts himself so that he
Has earned the title "First Rate?"

I know such a man and so do you,
Who fits the description above.
A man whose steps are ordered by God,
Whose motive, quite simply is love.

When John is called someday to heaven
"Well done!" He'll hear them say.
"That's fine with me," John will reply,
"I'll cook 'em right away."

To Larry Piper

We're gathered today to honor this man
Who walked through life with a definite plan,
He helped all the athletes at Danville High
For thirty long years: What an all-around guy!

He was always available to help those in need,
He's accomplished many an unheralded deed,
He'd stop what he was doing and say, "I'll do it."
He'd cheer the downhearted with, "You can go through it."

When we were with Larry in public places,
He always responded to familiar faces,
He'd break out a grinnin', he really was pleased
To hear someone holler, "Hello, there, Ease!"

Many who knew him would stop him to say,
"Thank you for helping me; I remember that day."
I know he has influenced many a teen
To stay on the right track and not make a scene.

Here in his church, in his favorite place,
We remember his reverence and the smile on his face.
He often shared stories of what Jesus had done,
How the Lord fought his battles, and how he had won.

Larry loved God and it showed in his life,
He loved all his family, especially his wife,
He loved all of us gathered in here today,
And if Larry could speak, he'd probably say:

"If only you people could all see me now,
There's no pain in my body, no sweat on my brow,
What I'm asking of you, in my heart so sincere;
Make arrangements today to meet me up here."

(This was a eulogy I wrote and read at Larry's funeral.)

To Ben Miller, My Neighbor, Cousin, and Friend

Years ago, I lived next door
To the Miller clan, you see.
Kathryn and I were very close,
Like two sisters then were we.

Ben was busy with his life
Doing mischief here and there,
But sometimes he would as my mom,
"Grace, would you please cut my hair?"

He had a dog named Tarzan
And treated him like a baby,
But one day he asked my dad,
"Please shoot him. He has rabies."

I felt so sad for Ben that day,
My dad felt sorry too.
But when a dog gets that disease,
That's all that you can do.

Years flew past, we all grew up,
And went our separate ways,
We'd see each other now and then,
And share things about our days.

Ben used to work at a grocery store
Where often I would shop,
He'd meet me with a friendly smile
And often he would stop.

To share with me about his life,
Or talk about our folks,
He'd make me laugh so very hard
At one of his funny jokes.

Then troubled times frustrated Ben,
But we won't dwell on that.
God so faithfully intervened,
And today, look where Ben is at!

Serving God has been worthwhile,
He's given Ben a whole new life,
New hope, new dreams, a brighter smile,
And blessing of blessings, a beautiful wife.

To an Old Friend

You know you are old without being told,
When wearing a girdle's not worth it,
The middle age spread is already ahead
So why should you bother to girth it?

You know you are "there" when you no longer wear
Tight fitting jeans with a sweater.
And you can't pass a mirror without saying "Dear,
You're not getting older, just better."

You're over the hill when your energy's nil,
And "gay" is a positive feeling.
You're ripe for the grave, when you no longer crave
The excitement of wheeling and dealing.

You know you're antique when you grow sad and weak
Each year when your birthday rolls around,
And you fly in a rage when your kids tell your age
A sure sign you're the Medicare-bound!

So, as you engage in the battle with age,
Remember the good years you've had.
Take time to consider the alternative's bitter.
Getting old is no really that bad!

From one who knows!

Family Reunion 1957

Now if you've had enough to eat,
Please listen for a while,
I'd like to have attention please,
Come on now, let's all smile.

No fair, Uncle Johnny,
Get your feet from under the table,
And you, dear Aunt Edith,
Get up, if you are able.

Well, hello now Uncle Gus,
How's everyone out your way,
Whaddya know there's Uncle Bill,
What have you got to say?

And Grandma Richie, how are you,
Looking younger all the time,
And there's my Uncle Lester just
A listenin' to this rhyme.

Hope you all are feeling well
And having lots of fun,
I hope the last year has
Been good to each and every one.
Hi! Aunt Lizzie, glad you're here;
Say, Jonie's quite a lady,
Hey, Granddad, how's it feel
To be almost eighty?

Now quit your laughing, Uncle Doc,
What's the matter with my dress?
I wore it so the food I ate
Would have more room to digest.

That Norman Hawkins sure can eat,
But this one thing I'll say,
His kisses are like vitamin pills,
I get just one—a-day.

Seriously now, we've had our fun,
And I would like to say
I'm thankful to the Lord above
That you all came today.

As we gather here today
This prayer is on my heart,
That on that great reunion day,
We'll meet to never part.

Another Family Reunion 1958!

Come on now folks and gather around
While you settle your fabulous dinner,
I'm sure that after all of that food,
We'll none of us get any thinner.

Listen closely and you will hear
About our family tree,
How it has grown a little bit more
And yet, as you all can see…

We're missing two whom we all adored,
But this one thing I know,
That none of us will ever forget
Our own Janice and Uncle Joe.

Reunions are a happy time
When all of us are here,
But when we see an empty place
We all have to shed a tear.

But let's thank God abundantly
For blessings he has given,
And if we never meet on earth,
Let's pray we'll meet in Heaven.

Family Reunion 1992

I don't like reunions, and that's a known fact,
But I've started my poem, without any tact!
Please let me explain (Now hold that mean look!)
The truth of the matter is—I HATE TO COOK!

All of you ladies are Pillsbury's best,
But culinary art is NOT where I'm blest,
Not even one person wants my recipe,
(Of course, it's available at old KFC!)

And yes, I bring Twinkies (Kids dearly love 'em.)
Do I take home the extras? There's rarely any of 'em.
I've done you a favor by not bringing much
That bears forth the flavor of Norma's own touch.

Now, let me get serious a minute or two,
I'll try to explain reunions to you:
We meet in a park on a scheduled date,
With food in our baskets to fill every plate.

We get reacquainted with some we forgot,
And meet the new members of our family lot.
Then, suddenly, we see empty places
Where once sat our loved ones with smiling faces.

And pain cries out within my breast,
For those whom our family have laid to rest.
In that sad moment, I then realize
That Jesus shall soon split Eastern skies.

And those whose sins have been forgiven
Shall rise to meet Him in God's sweet Heaven.
Such a reunion on that golden shore
With those of our family who've gone on before!

That's one reunion I don't want to miss,
But before I close, let me say this…

I hope to see you all there!

To Two Radiation Techs for Breast Cancer

Thank you, guys, for your dedication
To such a worthwhile occupation,
Your knowledge, skills and gentle ways
Helped me survive these stressful days.

While I lay on that cold, hard table
I prayed to God, who is **SO** able,
To direct each "beam" to where it could
Kill **all** the bad and protect the good.

I won't miss coming here every day,
But this one think I truthfully say—
You guys take what is often tragic
And give it a touch that's almost magic.

God Bless you

Ode to 4457 Hospital Nurses

All of you nurses are blessed by God,
Helping those among whom you daily trod,
Following directions by the letter!
Determined to make us all feel much better.
Always smiling and working with speed
Making certain to meet our every need.
I can't say I'm happy to spend time here,
But each of you has been such a dear,
And whatever day I'm allowed to depart,
Thankfulness to *all* of *you* will be in my heart!

Ode to Wallace

I had never heard of Wallace
Or of its Highway Band,
Until a good friend told me,
"They're the best one in the land."

So she drove me down to Wallace
One pleasant summer night,
And at once I was persuaded
That my friend was oh, so right!

The singers and musicians
Really bless the country sound,
The food was so delightful,
And Tony's pie was just profound.

Several times I played with them
A memory time cannot erase.
I played some songs on keyboard,
And once or twice on bass.

What a way to spend an evening!
What good music, food, and friends!
Wallace has become to me
A favorite place where "lonely" ends!

To My President Bush 43

You seem to have chosen a road not taken,
For never before has our land been so shaken
By a terrorist act of such magnitude,
And war with an enemy so godless and crude.

Then came Katrina and gross devastation,
And the increasing problem of immigration,
Large corporations are reducing in force,
Pension plans are canceled without recourse.

Medicare concerns and Asian bird flu
Must be perplexing and stressful to you.
Social Security requires much deep thought,
And Home Security is with anxiety fraught.

Such a brief list of all the crises you face,
But remember! God chose you to be in this place.
Here is a fact recognized by your fans,
The deadliest enemies attacking your plans

Are the negative people, media backed?
Whatever you endeavor, they will attack.
By lies and omission they seek to destroy
The strategies, thoughts, and plans you employ.

We pray for you daily that God will renew
Your strength and your wisdom in all that you do.
We've watched you age quickly under the stress,
But we are confident that our God will bless.

Don't be discouraged by what seems to be
Still another attack on uncharted sea,
Keep believing in God and His plan for your life.
That MAJORITY love you AND your beautiful wife.

Where would we be in our country today
If the negative people did things their way?
We thank God for giving us a God-loving man
Who serves as President of our beloved land.

Little Robin Redbreast

(This is the first poem I ever wrote. Our teacher read poetry to us and asked our fourth-grade class to each write a poem. I've been writing poetry ever since.)

Little robin redbreast,
Singing in a tree,
Though very early in the year,
She's as happy as can be.

She flies about from tree to tree,
And then she builds her nest
In the choiciest place she's found,
She's sure it will be the very best.

Soon in the nest will be
Four tiny effs of blue,
Then count the weeks, 1, 2, 3,
There'll be baby birdies too.

When baby birdies hop around,
And mother bird a worm has found,
Then they see what she has brought,
They forget the manners they've been taught.

On their first winter,
They fly to the south,
And when they come back,
They'll feed their own mouth.

Holidays

New Year 1951

A New Year, a new leaf,
Another year gone by!
Could we but see God's record,
Would we shout or would we sigh?

Has this past year been a blessing?
Have we stood through every test?
Have we helped to save a sinner?
Or did we leave it to the rest?

Did we help to cheer the weary?
Did we lend a helping hand?
Did we grasp each opportunity
To tell salvation's plan?

Did we go to every service,
Both to church and Sunday School?
Were we faithful in our tithing?
Did we live by the Holy rule?

Or, did we in 1951,
Fail to find our given place?
Did we leave our work for others
Being too tired to run the race?

When Jesus spoke and told us
To speak to someone dear,
Did we do as we were bidden?
Or did we linger back in fear?

Did we as Christian people
Fill the year up to the brim
By always living in God's will
Doing things to glorify Him?

Have we kept our lights all shining?
Have we always testified?
Have we stood before the worldly,
Steady in God, even though tried?

The year of 1951
Isn't as it could have been.
We have often failed our heavenly father,
But we can't go back again.

We'll have to work much faster,
For not long will we be here,
Jesus' coming draweth closer
When God's own Son will appear.

We must keep our eyes to heaven,
Lest we stumble and fall flat,
Lest we lose our home in glory
And from his mouth are spat.

Stop and think about the past year;
Check up on yourself tonight,
Then ask God's forgiveness
And start the New Year out all right.

The Meaning of Easter

'Twas on this day so long ago,
That Jesus paid the cost,
He died alone on Calvary
That we would not be lost.

God gave His Son to die for us
On the fatal day of yore,
He died in agony and pain
As our sin and shame, he bore.

So, think not of Easter hats,
Or pretty clothes to wear,
But think of Easter as a day
For Christian joy to share.

Go to church and Sunday School,
And be not dressed in vain,
But think of Him who died for us,
Then get down and pray again.

Death Defeated

Brown, cold earth is
Frosted with a light coat
Of Green.
Tender shoots
Tentatively emerge
Into the warmth of the spring sun.
Nearby,
A tomb,
Holding death in its being,
Is approached
By an angel,
Who speaks.
Life comes forth!
Christ lives!
The earth greens,
Shoots spring buds
Which burst forth
In full Bloom—
Hope reigns.
Death is defeated.

This Is the Day

Being a mother is life's greatest perk,
It's an emotional time filled with pleasure and work,
A roller-coaster ride of fast ups and downs,
A mysterious box jammed with smiles and frowns.

It's an exciting journey with countless detours,
Sometimes confronting frightening features,
It's a comedy show with laughter and fun,
Or a tragic drama that leaves you undone.

Look around you today, you'll probably find
Mother and grandmas who have worried minds,
Because of a problem at this time in their life,
It's no easy matter to be a mother and wife.

There's no guarantee on your great wedding day
That all will be well, and everything okay.
Without God to help us through troubles and woes
How would we make it? Only God knows.

Yes, there's contentment, happiness, joy,
Then heartaches and grief sneak in to destroy,
Before you're aware of it, everything's now changed
In spite of whatever you've already arranged.

A child becomes ill, and you're worried so much,
Your teen is rebellious and shrinks from your touch,
Your husband is laid off from the place where he works,
There's now no more income and poverty lurks.

Then baby gets better and what sweet relief!
Your obstreperous teen has embraced your belief,
Your husband's new job is an answer to prayer,
You realize anew that God really does care.

Then come more trials that rob you of breath,
You're facing disease, disaster, or death,
You fall on your knees and tell God all about it,
He'll be right beside you, don't ever doubt it.

I remember today all the past many years
That are loaded with sunshine, laughter and tears,
I can honestly say that God is so good,
He's worked everything out as I knew He could

Don't regret trials that help you to grow
Closer to Jesus, for someday you'll know
That all things do work together for good
When we trust Him completely, the way we should.

This is the day that the Lord hath made,
We will all face it and not be afraid,
Loving and trusting the Lord is our choice,
And in spite of what happens, we will rejoice.

Being a Mother

Mothers, God has given you
A special kind of job to do,
One that even He can't fill,
One requiring unique skill.

You must take a tiny life,
And shelter it from harm and strife,
You must nurture it in love
With strength and courage from above.

You must feed and clothe and train
The child who in our arms has lain
And pray for him each night and day,
And teach him of God's holy way.

You must watch with anxious eye
When he's sick, his fever high.
And when he doesn't understand
You must gently hold his hand.

You must know just what to say
When bumps and bruises come his way,
And when he has to make a choice,
You must tell him, "Heed God's voice."

Then, when years have swiftly flown,
You must admit your child has grown,
And sadly watch him walk away.
"God Bless You, Child," you smile and say.

Then, you turn to God and ask,
"Do you call that an impossible task?
I'd not trade jobs with any other,
There's no greater job than being a mother."

A Tribute to Mother

Mother's Day comes once a year,
We bring her gifts and flowers,
But I love Mother every day,
All the minutes, all the hours.
I thank God for giving me
A mother like my own,
And most of all, I thank the Lord,
For the love that she has shown.

I love you, Mother,
And I want you to know,
I love you Mother,
Though it doesn't always show,
I thank you, Mother,
For simply being you,
For without you, Mother,
Whatever would I do?

Many are the times I'm sure
When I've caused your tears to flow,
Many are the hours you've spent
In prayer for me, I know,
And though you'd not admit it,
I've brought you misery,
I thank the Lord for you, dear Mom,
You mean SO MUCH to me.

To Mom from Chris, My Son

Mother,
I wanted to take this time to tell you how special you are.
You have always been there for me,
To encourage me in all that I have done,
You have picked me up when I have fallen,
And encourages me to go on,
You have supported me when others haven't,
And always take me to God,
I never seem to take the time,
To tell you how I feel,
But I will always love you.

My brother and I though seldom tell,
Have always followed your leading,
Even in the education
That sometimes have come with screaming.

On this Mother's Day I wanted you to know
This one thing is for sure
I will never be a poet
For this I'm only dreaming!

My Mother

There is one, whom I hold dear,
And I'd like for you to know,
She's the girl who married Daddy
So many years ago.

Then, her hair was blacker
Then the darkest, blackest night,
But since she's raised our family,
It is slowly turning white.

When I was but a baby
I recognized her touch,
I could tell the way she held me,
That she loved me very much.

Many were the hours
That she spent on my behalf.
And many were the antics
She went through to make me laugh.

Swiftly, time rolled onward
And I grew with every day,
Mom was always there to guide me,
Lest I fell along the way.

I remember how she sacrificed
So I might have a dress,
How she never seemed to mind it
When she ended up with less.

Oh, yes and I remember,
How her eyes filled with delight,
When I did a chore unbidden,
When I did what she thought right.

Then, although I loved her
I never tried to show
That to me she is the dearest
Of all mothers that I know.

But now I'm going to make up
For the things I've left unsaid.
How I love you lovely Mother!
May God bless your years ahead.

And now that I'm a mother
I shall be quite satisfied,
If I am half the mother
As the one here at my side.

Celebrate

Today we celebrate
Mom's homegoing
To be with her Lord,
Whom she loved so much.
This is the day she longed for
With joyous anticipation.
This is the day she prepared for
By being a Godly example.
We mourn not for her,
But for ourselves.
She would say to us,
"Celebrate! Celebrate!
I've finished my course,
I'm going home."
We don't understand
The suffering
She endured at the end,
But we know beyond doubt
That today Mom does not
Remember the pain, so
Celebrate! Celebrate!

Memories of My Mom

Written by my brother Larry Tellier

I first met my mom,
In nineteen forty-three,
The year I was the fifth,
To join the family tree.

Kids don't remember much,
Of the first few years you see,
So, I will first relate,
Some things she passed to me

She told me of a time,
During my first year of life,
When I was so long cranky,
And she was filled with strife.

She called upon the Lord,
And asked his help that day,
While she promised to be faithful,
Until she passed away.

She said she'd keep her kids,
In church while they grew up,
And to lead them to the Lord,
In which she needed more than luck.

She kept each of the promises,
She made to him that day,
And followed in his footsteps,
As he showed her the way.

If you look beside her bed,
At the carpet on the floor,
You'll see two small depressions,
From her knees at heaven's door.

There she asked the Lord for mercy,
And guidance from above,
For each one in her family,
And for everyone she loved.

As time passed by so quickly,
And I grew from boy to man,
There are things I remember,
That I'll relate as best I can.

I cannot count the times,
I passed Mom's bedroom door,
And heard her voice come through it,
As her heart she would outpour.

My name was often mentioned,
Along with others here today,
Whose problems always concerned her,
Each time she knelt to pray.

She believed the Bible fully,
She knew each line and verse,
And as she read it over and over,
It was as if it were the first.

She read it to her children,
And taught them wrong from right,
As she guided each one's path,
And led their prayers at night.

Have you ever criticized,
One who has done you wrong?
Mom was the one who never,
Her faith helped her along.

Her faith was always steadfast,
Stout as an old oak tree,
And the example that she set,
Is what we should strive to be.

To keep her family together,
She became the glue,
But now that she's passed from us,
What are we to do?

We have one hope left to us,
And that's on him above,
We give our thanks unto him,
For giving her—to us—to love.

A Tribute to Dad
(Clement Tellier)

Some kids may call him father,
And others call him Dad,
But I'll praise the Lord forever
That he gave me the best one He had.

My dad was always a hero,
Why, he could fix anything,
He could put my world back together
With a little glue and string.

He was taller and stronger than any,
He was wiser than any I knew,
Of course, there was many a fight
With those who thought it not true.

Why, he could do anything better
Than all the rest of the dads,
And he was much better looking
Than the daddies of other lads.

My daydreams of childhood are altered
But my thoughts of Dad were all true,
He's still the best of all daddies
And he's still nice looking too.

He's still the dad of my childhood,
He'll be the same Dad tomorrow,
And though I'm no longer a youngster,
He stands by me in joy or sorrow.

I now can truly be thankful
That he was so narrow and strict,
For I know that today I'm a Christian
By the tune of the hickory stick.

And so on this day, today,
I'll thank the Father above
That he gave me a wonderful father
To honor, cherish, and to love.

Dad's Call

One April day
Dad was called away,
He'd been working hard
In the yard
All afternoon;
But soon
He tired.
He'd retire
For the night he thought.
But God sought
To claim his soul
While it was whole
And fresh from prayer;
Dad walked to where
The car awaited.
He hesitated…
Perhaps knowing
He was going
Forever.
God never
Withdrew His claim.
He'd called Dad's name,
And being brave,
Dad faced the grave
With one quick breath
And feared not death

Nor dying;
But we, crying…
Left in grief,
Found relief
In knowing
Dad's going
Was carefully planned
By God's hand.
Amen.

Dad's Eulogy

(I wrote and read this at Dad's funeral.)

Various records will reveal that Clement E. Tellier was born in Danville, Illinois, on December 15, 1909, son of Clement A. and Eva Pichon Tellier. He is survived by his wife, Grace Richardson Tellier, six sons: Ronald, Robert, Allan, Larry, Dan and Dwight; one daughter, Mrs. Norman (Norma) Hawkins; nine grandchildren and one great-grandchild. He has four brothers: Andrew, Louis, William, and Leland. He was preceded in death by his parents, two sisters, and three brothers.

Other records will verify that Daddy was a mine manager, farmer, construction worker, and a heavy equipment operator for the State Highway Department.

But today, we'd like to share with you friends and loved ones here, those things about Daddy that the records don't tell you.

Daddy love to be out-of-doors. When we asked his brothers, cousins, sons, and grandsons what they would like to share, they each said that the times they spent hunting and fishing with him were the most valued memories. Even though they didn't always bag or catch anything, they still enjoyed the times spent with him.

Another thing about Daddy that records won't show is that he had a keen sense of humor. Many of you here have been the victim of his practical jokes. On the other hand, many of you have enjoyed "getting on back" on him. His collection of humorous cards and cartoons which people have sent to him, mostly anonymously, is famous.

Daddy was a teacher too. Oh, you won't find a certificate to verify this, but ask any of his kids. He taught us to take pride in hard work, to be honest and trustworthy, to develop a common sense and apply it to everyday situations. He taught us to swim, fish, drive a car, and to handle weapons safely.

Daddy doesn't hold a degree for guidance counselor, but many times his ability to advise us kids has changed the course of our lives. Once, when one of us had reached a decision to leave home, Dad came to him, not knowing of this decision, and the son stayed and a week later, gave his heart to the Lord. He gives partial credit to Daddy for the fact that he's was in the ministry later. An important aspect of Daddy's guidance was in keeping silent and accepting our decisions as final when he felt we had carefully considered our situation. He never interfered unless we asked him to.

Today, Daddy is doing the same as he's always done for us—leading the way—going before, unafraid of what lies ahead. We mourn for ourselves today because we know that Daddy is with the Lord. We cannot mourn that he saw Jesus before we did. We would not wish him back among us to pick up again his earthly worries, his aches and pains. So, with heavy hearts, but confident hope, we're just saying goodbye to Daddy for a short time.

As Christians we know we will see him again. Until then, "Goodbye for now, Daddy."

Squeeze Play

The ghosts are hardly vanished
Nor the goblins out of sight,
'Til the gaily ringing Christmas bells
Advertise the coming night.

The cats are hardly scattered
Nor the witches laid away,
'Til ol' Santa and his reindeer
Are assembled on display.

But it still remains a mystery
Why a land that's blessed so much
Has crowded out Thanksgiving
With its humble, grateful touch.

We're so busy looking forward
To the gifts and fun we've planned
That we forget to say a thank you
For the blessings in our hand.

Wouldn't it be wonderful
If people would remember
That Thanksgiving is the holiday—
At least, until December?

Thanksgiving Day

Thanksgiving Day has come and past,
Why must time go so awfully fast?
We've had a lovely time today,
Plenty of food and time to play.

Chicken and dressing and a whole lot of cake,
Pies and pudding all a different make,
We also had noodles, yum, yum, yum,
You can be sure that I did eat some.

The sauce was delicious, cranberry, you bet,
Each of the family a bite they did get,
The only drawback was dishes piled high,
When time to wash 'em, each drew a deep sigh.

One by one, they had to sit back,
And let their food go down its right track,
But still they were talking, not able just to sit,
Each telling some gossip, and absorbing each bit.

But with dishes over and all put away,
The women talking, each one had to say,
"The dinner was lovely, but I ate too much,
The meal stood out clearly in Grandma's own touch."

Thanksgiving 1954

I come to Thee with humble heart
To thank You, Lord, today,
For love, you did to me impart,
For teaching me to pray.

For giving peace deep down inside,
For your word to guide my way,
And especially for the One who died,
I thank Thee, Lord, today.

For every heartache, every trial
You've allowed to come my way,
For every joy and every smile,
Thank You, Lord, I say.

Thank Thee, Lord, not just today,
But all year long as well,
For keeping me in the narrow way,
For guarding me from hell.

Help me, oh Lord, to ever be
Thankful enough to say,
"Take my life, oh Lord, to Thee,
And lead me where you may.

Thankful enough to do your will,
To go where you'd have me go,
Thankful enough to love Thee still
When tears of sorrow flow.

Thankful enough to sacrifice."
I ask myself this day.
Thankful enough to give my life:
Yes! Help me, Lord, I pray.

Thanksgiving 2016

I thank you, Lord, almost everyday
That I was born in the USA!
In spite of our troubles and situations,
I'm glad I live in this super nation!

I'm thankful, Lord, for the husband you gave
And the sixty years shared before his grave,
Thank you, Lord, for the two sons we had
Who both matured proudly just like their dad.

Thank you, Lord, for the friends we share,
Like those here today who show that they care,
And people who try hard to meet all our whims.
What would we do today without them?

Thank you, Lord, for giving your life,
Providing for us an escape from our strife
And a retirement plan that's Heaven above,
Because of your death, because of your love.

Looking for Christmas

I looked into each passing face,
In every unexpected place,
But couldn't seem to find a trace—of Christmas.

I gazed intently at the snow
And at a snowman—What a show!
It was evident he didn't know of Christmas.

I searched around the Christmas tree,
And in each gift shop I could see,
But none was of much help to me. Where's Christmas?

So, then I thought of Santa Claus,
He should surely know because
Folks give to him so much applause at Christmas.

But when I asked him, I could see
He didn't know how to answer me,
So, I walked on with but one plea—where's Christmas?

Then suddenly from the dark of night,
I saw a bright and shining light
That seemed to tell me that it might know where's Christmas

And with the shining of the star
I saw a manger scene afar
That seemed to beckon, "Here we are, here's Christmas."

Then I knew without a doubt
That I would find the answer out,
Something in me seemed to shout, "Here's Christmas."

Then Christ spoke sweetly into my ear,
"You'll find Christmas very near,
For Christmas is way down in hear—in the heart."

Christmas in the USA

It's Christmas in the USA,
And how thankful we should be
That we can come to church today
In a land that's rich and free.

A land where we can worship God
And read His Holy Word
And follow in the path He trod
Where blessed hymns are heard.

How glad we are for America
And for the red, white, and blue,
And especially for Christianity
And a Christmas season too.

Many there are in this world today
Living in dark despair,
No Christmas day to they celebrate,
No Christmas spirit there.

Of the Christ child born in the manger
These millions have never been told,
They were born in a heathen land
Where sin has taken hold.

So, we who know what Christmas is,
Are selfish if we don't try
To spread the word to those lost souls
Who are sick and not ready to die,

To those who are weary
And tired of this life,
Who are tired of the shame
And sickened by strife.

We hold these flags in our hands today
To remind you everyone,
That are truly so fortunate
Because we know God's only son.

An Eternal Gift

Symbols of Christmas crowd our view
Throughout the month of December,
Beautiful trees and elaborate lights
Help each of us to remember.

That awesome night so long ago
When Christ was born in a manger,
Oh, what a gift—this precious young baby
Became to each seeking stranger.

The prophet Isaiah foretold of His birth
For this was the Savior of man,
Bu he was despised and rejected by some
Who refused to accept God's plan.

Oh, what a gift—this Son of God,
Who was born to die for our sin!
But unlike the gifts found under the tree
It shall ever remain within.

This gift has given me life evermore,
A life filled with purpose and love,
Because of this gift that He's given me.
I can someday meet Him above.

One Gift Forgotten?

I have my gifts all wrapped with care,
Placed beneath my tree so gay,
I've planned a festive time so fair
To take place this Christmas Day.

I've spent much time in buying
For each one on my list,
And after much wrapping and tying,
I'm sure not one I've missed.

I've been in every store in town,
Now that's just fine, I guess,
But I've had a time just getting around
In such a crowded mess.

I've even bought my postage stamps,
My cards are in the mail,
All over town are Christmas lamps
This merry time to hail.

But hark? The Herald Angels sing,
Or can you hear the song?
The message that the angels bring
Can cheer the weary throng.

God's gift to us was His own Son,
What can we give to show
We're truly glad for what He's done
Because He loves us so?

God wants a gift from each of you
To prove we love our Lord,
What more is there that we can do,
Than to pray and read His word.

I'm going to consecrate myself anew
I know He'll be so glad!
Why don't you give Him your heart too?
Someday you'll wish you had.

Christ's Gift List to Christians

Listen, my children, I have something to say,
As you're making great plans for this Christmas Day:

It is my birthday, you all will agree,
Well, here's my wants—from you to me.
It won't set you back; put your money away,
What I want you to give is more time to pray.

Show more compassion to those who have needs,
Share what you have in faith and in deeds,
Remember those watching you, know you are mine,
So be a true witness of the exemplary kind.

Also, I'd like to bask more in your praise,
I'd like less complaining about bad-hair days.
Near the top of my list (and I'll hold you all liable)
I want you to read and really study the Bible.

Oh, yes, I need you so send up more prayer,
Quite trying to solve problems, knowing I'm there.
A "must have" on my list, is for you to be sharing
My message of love, of forgiveness and caring.

I want your clean hearts that delight in my word,
When you give me these things, I'll know I've been heard.

Merry Christmas from the Birthday Child,
And Soon-Coming King, Jesus

Meaning of Christmas

Christmas began with a brilliant star
That was seen by the shepherds that night
When angels announced the birth of a babe
As they sang mid a heavenly light.

What a wonderful gift this Christ child is
Who was sent from the Father above
To extend His good will and peace on earth,
And to prove to mankind His great love.

Yet many today do not seem to know
Or, they know, but they seem uncaring
That the meaning of Christmas really is
Not in receiving but sharing.

Teacher and Her Students

(Student names are fictitious and refer to characteristics of student personalities observed.)

The Class of '49

Can you believe it's been fifty years
Since our graduation from OTHS?
Do you remember your dreams back then?
We all had some pretty big ones, is my guess.

We were the class who would change the world,
Increase the potential of the human race,
Create ideals from our fertile brains
That would make our planet a much better place.

We set forth with plans in '49,
And often exceeded our ultimate dreams,
We become spouses, parents, and doers
Of what could be labeled "impossible" schemes.

Boldly we blazed new, challenging trails
That led to various countries and towns,
Wherever we went, whatever we did—
We were not defeated by the ups and downs.

Teachers, nurses, and builders were we
Who emerged to perform that which we had planned,
Engineers, farmers, and a minister, too,
All eager to serve, to provide, to command.

And serve, we did, and provided, and led,
Fulfilling a dream we had dreamed long ago.
Of making our world a better place,
Well, we actually did it, don't you know!

I'm so glad to be part of this class
Whose greatest, outstanding source of pride
Lies not in career or material gains
But in your children, and the spouse at your side.

As we face uncertain times ahead
May God grant us the strength to continue on—
Living life to the fullest extent,
Relishing, anticipating each new dawn.

I challenge each of you reading this
To make the same careful preparation
For the rest of our life and, yes, beyond,
What you did for high school graduation.

I Am a Teacher

Treading softly, yet with confidence and authority,
Along the curious recesses of vulnerable minds,
Challenging dormant abilities to exceed previous boundaries,
Provoking questions that demand consideration
And sometimes, solutions,
Exposing truths which shall remain forever unchanged,
Assessing others which are temporal.
Stepping lightly among tender lives,
Bending, stretching here and there to touch,
Sharing my humanness, my entity,
Absorbing the fulfillment within me brought on by
The upward thrust of their seeking minds
That surge with energy and curiosity,
Participating in their agonies and accomplishments

For I am a Teacher.

I Am

An advocate of
Truth
A support for
Those who
Must learn
A help for
Helplessness
A smile for
Those without
A Reason to
Smile,
An inspiration for
Those in complacency
I am a Teacher!

Our Principal

A leader is one who leads by example,
Who is not afraid of unknowns,
He willingly charts the uncharted paths,
He overlooks no unturned stones.

A leader will tackle what has to be done,
Not asking of anyone else
The task of completing difficult jobs
That he's never done himself.

A leader will handle with wisdom and care
The people who follow his course,
He won't abuse his power of office,
He governs with fairness, not force.

Such is the man we are honoring today,
A leader of whom we are proud,
A man whose example speaks for itself,
A man who stands tall in the crowd.

And so, Larry, we dedicate this,
Our concert, in honor of you,
We sing and play forth a tribute today,
You'll remember your whole life through.

To Mary, My Teacher Friend

*(Mary and her husband were having an open house
to celebrate their wedding anniversary, and all of the
school staff forgot. We were really embarrassed.)*

The hens wouldn't lay and the dog wouldn't stand,
The winds were too high and the planes couldn't land,
The sun wouldn't open and the clouds wouldn't close,
The kids had a fever and a cold in the nose,
Rain was predicted from east coast to west,
The stock market wobbled, and I couldn't invest,
There's war in Honduras, and crime in the street,
The Cards were winning, the Cubbies got beat,
School's about finished, there's so much to do,
The ax has descended; got rid of a few,
Grass has grown taller, stayed home to mow,
Fish were so hungry, had to feed 'em you know,
An old golfing buddy dragged me out by the heels,
Hair needs a cuttin', car's got no wheels,
To give more excuses, I'd really rather not,

The truth of the matter is…we just plain forgot.

To Don

(Don was killed in a wreck on Henning Road. He was a maintenance man at Westville schools.)

It's hard to accept that Donald has died,
He was such a neat person to know,
He worked in our district of number of years
And he smiled wherever he'd go.

He never complained about work to be done,
Though the job might sometimes be tough,
He'd make a remark to make us all laugh,
Then he'd finish that job, sure enough!

He fixed leaking pipes and stubborn machines,
But the job he loved best barring none—
Was taking good care of the football field
And our is now: Field Number One!

We're going to miss his knowledge and skills
How sad and depressing this seems,
But somehow we feel that Don is already
Planning his own "field of dreams."

Lost File

(I couldn't find a folder which contained some important information when I was teaching at Westville Jr. High. I had the school secretary put a notice in the daily bulletin. When I finally found it after asking everyone if they had seen it, I wrote this poem.)

Thank you, dear people for being so kind,
For helping me search for what I couldn't find,
The lost has turned up in an unusual place,
I'm certain there must be egg on my face,
Prob'ly an alien from a terrestrial station
Swooped into my room, and then growing bolder,
Ran to my desk and snatched up my folder.
Then hearing a noise at the 109 door,
He tossed my folder in the lower file drawer…

To the American Legion

Thank you so much for the flags that you gave,
Long o'er our schools may Old Glory wave,
May we ever remember the terrible cost,
The wars that were fought, the lives that were lost
By the foes of Old Glory, we've stood the test
Down through the decades of turmoil and strife
We've won by our courage our own way of life.
We look at the flag and salute it with pride,
Remembering our history and those who have died,
Remembering our past, but keeping in mind
Hope lies in the future, the past is behind,
And praying for wisdom to do what is right
To keep our flag waving and Old Glory in sight.

Subbing High School

The poor old lady who's subbing today
Knows nothing 'bout what's going down,
She probably sees us as immature teens
Who drive fast and party around.

I wonder if she ever tried out a drug,
Or if her life was broken and sad,
Did she have to worry when she arrived home
If she'd find both her mother and dad?

Did one of her close friends choose to die
Instead of facing life's situations?
Did she ever suffer the shame of abuse,
And that, by her family relations!

Would she understand if I tried to explain
How confusing my life seems to be?
But I do not know her and she's so much older,
How could she ever help me?

I know what they're thinking, I read their eyes,
I feel their confusion, their pressure,
Lord, how can I reach them and share your love
Which they need in infinite measure?

I'll say what I dare, and show them I care,
And pray for them throughout the day,
May they see Christ in this very old woman
Whenever they're looking my way.

Teens and I

They're full of fun and mischief too.
Smiles one minute, then angry or blue.

Bubbling over with super zest,
Then moving slowly, as though at rest.

Often happy and not knowing why,
Quick to temper, quick to cry.

Slow to listen to adult advice,
Sometimes nasty, but mostly nice.

Very friendly most of the time,
When around them long, then I'm

Apt to need a frequent break,
Still, I'll so gladly, eagerly take

The daily challenge they seem to be,
And I pray to God to enable me

To meet their needs, to understand
That teens and I walk hand in hand.

Nancy

There's fire in her eye
As Nancy strolls by,
I know she has pinned her next victim,
She'll never retreat
Nor admit a defeat,
That young lad will fall—per her dictum.

She'll flash him a smile
And giggle awhile
He'll blush and before he can answer
She'll turn with a bounce,
Give her long hair a flounce,
He'll gasp like a long-thirsted panther.

It's happened before
(According to lore)
Lorelie beckoned men to her rock,
Much to their surprise
Their ships were capsized,
None were able to sail to the dock.

Back to our Nancy
Who's caught Tim's fancy,
But he's quite unaware of her guile,
So needless to say,
She'll have bold way,
What a treasure she's caught with her smile!

Beware, gentle lad,
For soon you'll be sad,
Her heart is quite free, loose, and changing,
Walk on down the hall,
Don't give her a call,
Or your life she'll soon be deranging.

Just smile and say, "Hi!"
Then quickly pass by,
Unless it's a heartache you're wanting
If seeking a girl
Who'll give you a whirl,
Pick one who's sincere and less daunting.

Charlie

Look coming down the hallway!
Here's Charlie Jones, the clown,
He's wearing baggy trousers,
His hair is plastered down.

His smile is so contagious
Dispelling angst and gloom,
Each class becomes more friendly,
When Charlie's in the room.

I watch him as he studies,
And wonder if he knows
How he affects those 'round him,
No matter where he goes.

Although his grades are failing
He thinks he doing fine.
If he can create laughter
That's all that's on his mind.

Yes, Charlie's truly gifted
At making life more fun,
But is he ever worried
'Bout things he's never done.

What secret lurks beneath
His winning, winsome smile?
Is Charlie really happy
Or sad once in a while?

Joe

Joe sits by the window,
His eyes turn frequently in that direction,
His countenance, sober,
Involved in some life-changing introspection.
I'm curious. What thoughts
Has he unleashed for this moment's inspection?
Should I call his name or
Permit him to continue his reflection?
Am I interrupting
A problem he's trying to cope with somehow?
Is it needful that I
Get his attention focused on class—right now?
Why discourage thinking
About what only Joe knows? I will allow
A few more minutes
To solve his problems and smooth his troubled brow.
Does he feel set apart,
Disconnected from everyone around him?
Should I go stand near him?
Would my interference only confound him?
How else can I convey
That my concern and my caring surround him?
I'll be here to help him
Obliterate some of the woes that hound him.
Maybe Joe needs to know,
I see when he withdraws, but I understand.
If it were permitted,
At times like this, I would pray and hold his hand.
School code says: Be Careful.
So how can the gulf between us be spanned?
I sit back and watch Joe
And pray that he'll discover what God has planned.

Melinda

She stepped the hall with studied poise,
She flounced her long blond hair,
Bestowing smiles to all the boys
Who gravitated there.

Melinda's world was on cloud nine,
Her beauty, wealth, and brain
Assured her that her life was fine
'Til one day come the rain.

Her family seemed to fall apart,
Her father left her life,
Regardless of her broken heart,
He'd found another wife.

Today, Melinda walks the hall,
Her head bowed in despair,
No longer is she proud at all
About her gorgeous hair.

Her beauty fades a bit each day,
She smiles at no one now.
Her grades have fallen by the way,
I've got to help, but how?

The only thing I know to do
Is talk to God about it,
Melinda, I will pray for you,
Don't you ever doubt it!

Tom

Tom never just walks anywhere,
He'll strut, or sway, or prance,
I've never seen his shoulders slumped,
Nor malice in his glance.

With head held high, his chin straight out,
He claims the middle of the hall,
And those who swerve around him there
Don't seem to mind at all.

His smile is so perpetual,
To frown would break his stride,
Either he's the happiest kid
Or he fakes to save his pride.

The girls all love to gather near,
And vie for his attention,
He plays no favorites, I know,
To keep down the dissention.

Tom will strut until that day
A certain girl appears,
Then he'll have some shocking feelings
Like humility and tears.

Lord, help him walk with shoulders back,
Equipped to do all things,
That we require of men today,
In spite of what life brings.

Mary

Mary scrunches down through the hall,
Hoping to be unseen,
Clutching her books to her sagging breasts,
Her skin and clothes unclean.

Her eyes, downcast, acknowledge none,
Her shoulders slumped, spread doom,
She furtively glances right and left
Then slinks into a room.

Her desk, it seems, is at the back,
The closest to the door,
Unloading her books, she settles in,
And dreads what lies in store.

I smile and speak to her each day,
She never lifts her head,
As though not knowing what she should say,
She twists her hair instead.

When class begins, I know that she
Will never volunteer,
Whenever I chance to call on her,
I see her naked fear.

"What can I do to help?" I ask,
"I've tried so many things,
I'll smile, speak softly, and pray for her,
Before the last bell rings."

Narrative

The Green Pea Episode

This really happened when I was teaching at Westville Junior High. This incident earned me the title of "Green Pea Lady."

I went to lunch the other day,
Filled my plate in the same old way,
Started walking toward the door,
Bam! I suddenly hit the floor.

Potatoes and gravy were spilled around,
And, well, I was definitely down,
Wondering what had happened to me,
And then I saw IT, one green pea!

That pea was laughing, I declare!
Like all the students who were there,
Somehow I knew that pea had won,
As for my pride—now there was none.

Feeling like an awkward dude,
I hobbled up to get more food,
But now my foot began to swell,
Something was wrong, I could tell.

I barely made it to the room
The pain increased; Oh, gloom and doom!
I propped my foot up on a chair
And put an ice pack on it there.

But when I later tried to walk
It hurt so badly I had to balk,
The nurse said maybe I had better go
To get an x-ray so we would know

If I had broken a bone or not,
(By now it was hurting quite a lot)
The principal rolled me out
In my old black chair—quite a sight, no doubt!

But thank the Lord, nothing was broken,
And here I am, the doctor has spoken,
After two days on crutches, I'm very glad
To be back here. What a time I've had!

So ends my story, I swear it's true,
Those who saw it, will swear to it too.
I'll never forget what happened to me
The day I slipped on *one green pea*!

The Cup Incident

(This really happened with Dan and Dwight, my two youngest brothers. Our Grandmother gave them an old shaving mug.)

Oh, what a tale
Of two boys and a cup—
I know you'll accuse me
Of making it up.

It really did happen.
My story is true.
My two youngest brothers,
And Mom's in it too.

Now Gran had a mug
Which was old and chipped up
And she made the mistake
Of giving two boys one cup.

They fought from the moment
They both woke up
Over which one would drink
From the oversize cup.

They'd hide it the minute
The other was out—
In lamps, under chairs…
It was serious, no doubt.

Now Mother had taken
About all she could,
And she threatened to break it
And end it for good.

But they just didn't listen
To Mother's advice,
And soon they were at it
Once and then twice.

Mother had warned them
And now she was mad.
She grabbed it and slammed it
With all that strength she had.

The poor cup was broken,
But nothing was said.
Mom returned to her work
And the boys hung their head.

They picked up the pieces
In sweet harmony,
And placed them so gently
Where Mother could see.

They searched through the house
For a bottle of glue,
All the time talking peacefully
Of what they would do.

And when Mother came in
And saw what was up,
They were working so quietly
On the fought over cup.

They thanked her so sweetly,
Their eyes all alit,
For giving to them…
A Model Cup Kit!

Ice Cream Cones

*(The local paper wanted articles about ice cream experiences, and
I submitted this poem. It was published in the local paper.)*

The sun's so hot and I am too,
But I know what I'm gonna do,
I'll run down to the ice cream shop
And eat ice cream cones until I drop.
I just can't wait to wrap my tongue
Around a three dip chocolate one,
Or butterscotch or rocky road,
English toffee, or peach alamode,
Jamocha, lemon, sassafras,
Vanilla, praline, Oh, dear! Alas!
I'll never decide! Oh me! Oh my!
Someone tell me what kind to buy.
May I sample the sherbert, please?
And an itsy bite of the cherry cheese?
Raspberry, strawberry, grape and plum,
Marshmallow cream and bubble gum.
I simply must make up my mind
'Cause now I'm only third in line.
Blueberry, walnut or butter brickle,
Boy, boy! Am I in a pickle!
I've looked so long and tasted so many,
I think I'm full! I don't want any!

Agility Ability

Agatha Evelyn Virginia Meers
Can cross her eyes and wiggle her ears,
Scratch her head with her long slender toes.
Stretch her tongue to caress her nose.
Twist her elbows from inside to out
Stand on her hands and prance about
Crack her fingers and hold her breath
Until she scares her folks to death
Balance cups on the tip of her chin
While giving the world a mischievous grin
Sometimes I envy Agatha's agility
I would have fun with just half her ability.

Allison Betty Eats Spaghetti

There once was girl named Allison Betty
Who had such a hassle eating spaghetti,
She started by twisting her fork round and round
Until the spaghetti was all tightly wound
Then carefully she lifted the whole nervous mess
Up to her mouth, which was open no less,
Just at that moment, the spaghetti slid down

Onto the plate, the table, her gown
Bursting with tears of angry frustration,
She jabbed that spaghetti with determination,
Then picking it up with her ten little fingers
(Where even today the flavor still lingers)
She jammed it with vigor onto her tongue
'Til each string was swallowed one by one.

Sharing God's Gift

A poor little child in tattered clothes
Trudged slowly up the dirty street,
No one seemed to notice him there
Nor his ill-shod, twisted feet.

The hour was late and he must find a place
To rest on this winter eve,
But shelter was scarce on a night like this
And his tired body started to weave.

Just then a man with a kindly smile
Stopped and knelt in front of the youth,
"My child, you're alone and very cold.
I'll help you! I'm telling the truth."

The man took his hand and led him inside
To a room flooded with warmth and light,
"Sit down at the table and eat, my child,
Then we'll find you a bed for the night."

The little child's face glowed with happiness,
"Mister, you've made me so glad,
I'll thank you forever and always, sir,
For the best gift I've ever had."

Like that little child on the street that night
Many people are lost, without hope,
They carry a burden of sin and care
With no knowledge of how to cope.

We need to tell them about the child
Who was born in a Bethlehem stall,
How He lived, then died to save the world,
He was God's gift, the best gift of all.

Yes, God's gift to us, His beloved Son,
Just because He loved us so,
We must share Jesus with those in need
Whenever and wherever we go.

Dee Dee

(Dee Dee was a Pomeranian that we dearly loved!)

She was a beauty!
All fuzz and tail
About four pounds
Of love and fun
When I was down,
She seemed to know,
And she'd sit by my side
As if to cheer me up
And she did—
She was a member
Of our family
For fifteen years
And I mourned
When she died—
I mourned when she
Died.

What If?

(This happened at my church during a Wednesday night service. The raccoon fell through the ceiling of the balcony during the service.)

What if the raccoons who live up overhead
Decided to move to the sanctuary instead?
Can you imagine what a shock it would cause
To see raccoons with Bibles in their paws!

Or would they jump freely from pew to pew
And scare everybody, or at least a few?
Can't you just see their bright, beady eyes
Peering over the pulpit, much to Pastor's surprise?

Or maybe they'd rather sing out with the choir,
The result of that would no doubt be dire,
Or maybe they'd want to play the piano,
Boy, would our pianist ever get up and go!

What if they'd listen better than most,
Sensing the presence of the Holy Ghost,
Then maybe they'd say, (If raccoons could speak)
"You people here have what most people seek."

"We're just animals, from the Family Raccoon,
But we've heard today that He's coming soon,
Well, He's our creator as well as He's yours,
So let's live in peace. No more trap wars!"

Circus Time in Town

When it falls upon my ear
That the circus train is near,
Then I shake my piggy bank with all my might.
It is then that I regret
That my mother could not get
Me to save my money for the circus night.

So, at once I try to please,
And I remember not to tease,
So's my mom can see I'm really very good,
Why, I even sweep the floor,
And I do not slam the door,
So's to make sure that I'm clearly understood.

Daddy usually calls me pest,
But now I'm at my very best
He never even knows when I'm around.
Mother tries hard not to smile,
But she's thinking all the while,
"He's so good when it's circus time in town."

Then as the weeks roll by,
I give a long and worried sigh,
For my bank is still as empty as can be,
Though I take a peek each day,
To see if luck has come my way,
There is not a single cent for me to see.

By Friday, I am frantic,
And on Saturday in a panic,
Tonight's the night the circus comes to town,
All the guys will get to go,
They'll be there to watch the show,
And all at once the tears start coming down.

Now I didn't hear my dad
'Til he said to me, "Why lad,
Aren't you going with the fellows passing by?"
Then I sobbed my tale of woe,
"Well, I haven't any dough,"
And my father got a twinkle in his eye.

"If you'll not say a single word
About what I just overheard,
I am pretty sure there's money in your bank.
Now don't you say I told,
Or your ma is sure to scold."
And I jumped right up and charged him like a tank.

"You're the nicest Mom and Dad
That a fella ever had,
And I'll try my best to never let you down.
Now I've really got to run
Or I'll miss out on the fun
That I have when the circus comes to town."

Running Away

I was so mad one cold winter day
I said to my mother, "I'm running away."
She smiled and answered, "I'll help you pack
Your clothes and toys in a paper sack."

I looked to see if she really meant it,
This wasn't happening the way I intended,
She didn't cry or ask me to stay,
Or that if I did, I'd get me own way.

She fixed me a sandwich and a can of punch,
And said with a grin, "Enjoy your lunch."
I said "I'll show her," as I stomped out the door.
"She'll sure be sorry to see me no more."

"I'll get rich and famous. Then she'll see
What a mistake it was to be mean to me."
Many such comments I uttered that day
When I packed up my things and then ran away.

The farther I went, the slower I walked,
I'd said all I wanted, so I no longer talked,
The houses I passed were not ones I knew,
The names of the streets were peculiar too.

The wind picked up. I was getting cold,
A dog began barking, vicious, and bold,
Dropping my sack, I started to run,
"Someone please help," I cried. "Anyone?"

A tall, slender shadow stepped out from a tree,
There stood my mom, arms stretched out to me.
"Please, Mom," I cried. "I want to come back."
"Sounds good to me. I'll help you unpack."

Proud to Be an American

(I read this at church after 9/11, and our city mayor asked for a copy to take with him.)

September 11th
Has changed many things,
We all felt the fear
That world terrorism brings.

Our troops were trained and ready—
Often eager to leave
To defend our great nation
And what we all believe.

We're proud of our loved ones
Who are fighting a war,
They were willing to go
Where the tanks and guns roar.

They marched forth so bravely,
Determined, proud, and grim,
They knew with not a doubt
That they were going to win.

And win the war, they did,
With lightning-like speed
But the fighting continued,
Even more fiercely, indeed.

And last week, the capture
Of old Saddam Hussein
Revived their sagging spirits,
But the dangers still remain.

So Heavenly Father,
We fervently pray,
Protect our dear loved ones,
Send them home safe, one day.

We honor these families
For their sacrifice, too,
May they find strength and faith
By trusting in you.

So be with these families,
Give comfort and peace,
Knowing You will be with them
'Til all war shall cease.

A Clean Plate

I once had a friend called Caroline Kate
Who flatly refused to clean up her plate.
All she'd eat was what she like best,
(She'd dabble around with all the rest.)

She wouldn't eat carrots or black-eyed peas,
Or turnips or corn or beets, if you please,
She'd nibble her bread and leave all the crust,
But she gobbled desserts 'til she nearly would bust.

She filled up her plate with the biggest and best,
Then stir it up into an inedible mess.
"Why," said her mother, "don't you clean up your plate?
Indeed, 'til you do, I'll sit here and wait."

She waited an hour, a day, and a week,
But Caroline Kate had vowed not to eat.
The Fourth of July came and went by;
Still, they sat challenging, eye to eye.

The Halloween witches flew over the house,
Cackling in glee as they watched a wee mouse
Running and dancing all over the place
Of naughty, rebellious Caroline Kate.

Thanksgiving Day passed, and Christmas drew near,
Down Caroline's cheek spilled one wobbly tear,
"How can I write my Christmas wish
When I'm sitting here watching this awful dish?

"And how can I watch the Christmas parade
Or trim the tree with the pretties I've made,
Or hang up my stocking, or play in the snow,
Or skate on the ice when all the kids go…

I guess I'll just have to clean up my plate;
But look at this stuff," said Caroline Kate.
"I'll douse it with catsup and gulp it down fast!
I'll be free to leave this table at last."

So, gulp it, she did, and when she was done,
Her mother said to her, "Wasn't that fun!"
"Remember the next time; clean up your plate,
Or you'll get even longer, Caroline Kate!"

Indy 500 Mile

Calm is the wind and warm is the sun,
The 500 mile has just begun,
The pace car glides around the track
While drivers hold their racers back.

Slowly the pace car enters the pit,
The flag is down! This is it!
Powerful engines roar and whine,
The racers break the starting line.

A deafening cheer so strong and loud
Arises from the anxious crowd.
Afraid to watch, yet wanting to,
The wives stand up for a better view.

Suddenly, on the northeast turn
A car spins out and starts to burn,
Thousands scream, then hold their breath,
Will the driver burn to death?

The flagman waves the yellow flag,
Drivers slow down to a drag,
The ambulance hurries onto the track,
The driver's form is laid in back.

Then, from the stands, a woman's cry,
"Please, dear God, don't let him die!"
A wrecker tows the car away
As the drivers' wives begin to pray.

Drivers jam the pedals to the floor,
As once again the engines roar,
The wreck forgotten, the people smile—
Ready to watch the 500 Mile.

Ode to a Bug

(This happened in a large office I once worked in! It made a great big noise. I wrote the poem that night and put it on his desk the next day. He read to the staff.)

He chased the bug behind the desk
And vowed to kill the little pest,
So, with his great big size thirteens,
He squashed the bug to smithereens.
He breathed a sigh of deep content,
'Twas worth the energy he'd spent.

Here lies the bug who never knew
The damage that a shoe can do!

Waiting, Writing

(The local paper asked readers how we spent our times waiting on trains. I composed this poem while waiting on a train and sent it in. It was published in the Commercial News.*)*

Whenever I'm stopped by a slow-moving train,
I have a tendency to gripe and complain,
But that only makes the waiting seem worse,
'Til I finally decided to create some verse:
Without these cumbersome, slow-moving loads,
How many semis would be on the roads?
But there must be some method, however profound,
To channel this nuisance outside of our town!

Uncle Bones

*(I wrote this poem for my kids. It was also
read for a party at Liberty Estates.)*

The ghosts were all assembled
In a secret, hidden place,
It was dark and oh, so scary,
Not a smile on any face.

The leader stood before them,
His cheeks were pale and cold,
His eyes were sunken deeply
As this story he then told.

"My Uncle Bones related
This story long ago
About a little laddie
Whose name, I think, was Joe."

"He wouldn't mind his teacher
Nor his mamma nor his dad,
He teased the smaller children
And treated neighbors bad."

"He sassed and kicked and bellered
When his mama made him work
He slammed the door and walked out
With an evil, wicked smirk."

"He hid his mamma's slippers
And lost his daddy's tools.
He spilt the paint and cleaner
And made fun of all the rules."

"He threw such temper tantrums
And sometimes held his breath
Until he'd turn so purple,
That his folks were scared to death."

"Now Uncle Bones was watching
How Joey cried and wined,
And he thought he knew a method
That would teach that boy to mind."

"One night when Joe was sleeping
And the house was dark and still,
Uncle gained an entrance
Through an open window sill."

"He watched the boy a moment,
Then, as the clock struck two,
He grabbed up little Joey
And out the window flew."

"Uncle Bones won't tell me
What he did to little Joe,
He shakes his head and chuckles.
But this one thing I know…"

"You never saw a laddie
So quiet, good and kind,
And I'm sure you'll never meet one
Who's so quick and glad to mind."

"So, as I end my story,
I have one more thing to say,
Watch all the little children
At their work and at their play."

"And when you see a bad one,
You know just what to do,
Grab him by the collar
And make him go with you."

"And when you take him home again,
This fact I'll guarantee,
That ornery little critter
Will be as good as good can be."

Our Carnival Party At Liberty Estate Senor Citizen Apartments

Our Carnival Party was so much fun!
I'm sure you enjoyed it—yes, everyone!
There were challenging games, but we sure tried,
And when we won, it boosted our pride.
The numbered circle was quite an affair,
You just walked slowly to win a prize there!
But throwing six balls into three white jars
Demanded the skill of a person from Mars!
Now the game of golf had many winners
Who, because of their scores, enjoyed their dinners.
The tub full of ducks which were floating around
Afforded a prize if a number you found!
Three jars of candy were filled by a count,
To win one of these you just guessed the amount.

And, oh what delightful food was prepared,
No one left hungry, we all declared!

But most important, what I feel we must do
Is say Thanks from our hearts to all of you
Who planned ahead and made a way
For us to enjoy a GREAT CARNIVAL DAY!

A Memory

When I was four or five years old,
I seldom did what I was told,
But disobedience has a price
Which cost me dearly once or twice.

I went to town with Mom one day,
"Stay nearby," I heard her say.
"Don't wander around here by yourself,
And don't touch anything on a shelf."

Mom was busy doing her thing,
I took off like bird on the wing
To follow some laughing girls and boys
To the back of the store where there were toys.

Mom looked around and I was gone,
Instinct told her a search was on.
She told a clerk who helped her look
In every corner, aisle, and nook.

When they reached the back of the store,
(Where played a dozen kids or more)
My mother saw me, and at once
She ran and squeezed me in a crunch.

She swatted my bottom with her hand
Until I could just barely stand.
That's how I learned at five years old
To always do what I've been told.

My Vacation
Out of Bondage for a Whole Week

I had a week's vacation,
And I knew just where to go,
So, I got myself a suitcase
And I gathered up some dough.

I hopped aboard a diesel,
And I paid the man my fare,
Then I was set for Iowa
As we swiftly split the air.

The train stopped in Chicago,
So, I transferred to another,
I barely made the station
In time to catch the other.

Ah, then it was a streamline,
And I settled back to rest,
For now my senses told me
I was really headed west.

I tried to read a novel,
But it was to no avail,
As the lady sitting by me
Told a funny little tale.

At last, it was time for supper,
And I ordered quite a meal,
But to eat it was a nuisance
For the turning of the wheel.

I spilled the tea and water,
And I couldn't cut the meat,
And when I finally got a bite,
'Twas really, quite a feat.

Aunt Edith knew I'd be there,
So, she met me at the station,
I knew it would be lots of fun-
This hard-earned week's vacation.

With her two sons around me,
I laughed until I cried,
At their crazy jokes and antics,
And the funny pranks they tried.

And talk about the eating!
I gained three pounds in weight,
Fried chicken, corn, and ice cream,
You can be sure that I ate.

That week was surely shorter
Than the one that's just before,
Cause no sooner had I got there
Than the folks were at the door.

They all came out to get me,
And the weekend fairly flew,
Aunt Edith drove back with us,
Any my vacation was all through.

New England by Coach

Into the coach and down the road
The forty-three travelers sped
Ready to laugh and enjoy ourselves
And often we just slept or read.

Our first major stop was Niagara Falls,
How awesome! What power and might!
Driving on into Vermont was great
For the tree colors were truly a sight!

And, of course as we traveled
We heard funny stories and jokes
And many touching testimonies
From many thankful folks.

Yes, there were some embarrassing things
Such as Shirley's red-faced tale
And Larry was giving some candy away
That was supposed to be for sale.

New Hampshire, Maine-Here we come!
We tried lobster as was planned,
The entertainment was really top-notch,
We heard our own 3-man band.

We'll never forget old Provincetown
Where we watched as each whale hurls and twirls,
Where we walked the street for a place to eat,
And watched all the girls and girls.

We traveled through lots of other states,
We saw many interesting things,
We met some famous people, too,
And felt the joy that vacation brings.

But the best part of the trip to me
Is making new friends—like you,
I'll never forget your kindnesses,
Until next trip—adieu!

Opryland Hotel

It was the month before Christmas in Nashville town
When 52 friends and Lloyd drove down
To celebrate with and R&R
And Bus 44 beats driving a car.
So, off we went knowing full well
That when we got home, we'd have stories to tell.
Stories of humor and stupid mistakes
(Especially the one committed by Jake!)
And, yes we saw shows and beautiful sights
The greatest, perhaps, being the incredible lights.
We toured the old Ryman until about noon,
Then we all ate lunch at the Wild Horse Saloon,
We toured the town and saw lovely estates
Of stars well-known in the world and the States
And the Grand Old Opry on Saturday night
Turned our spirits on and our memories up bright,
One more comment as I finish this text—
"Gladys, please tell us—where are we going next!"

Gatlinburg

Fifty-six people climbed into the bus—
I mean—into the coach, please pardon us,
Eager to reach the Tennessee sun
And to make new friends with everyone.

In spite of the rain and mixed reservations,
We really liked Gladys's new preparations,
If life held no challenge—how boring, how dull!
So, we didn't mind these changes at all.

We're making memories each passing day—
Roger, you did this in a hilarious way!
Who can't forget your fruit-of-the-loom time
Or how Jake turned aside when you asked for a dime?

Touring the Biltmore makes me homesick to see
The beautiful mansion God's building for me.
That was some service we with Louis-
The music, the sermon blessed all who believe.

Paula, your comment to Gladys were classic,
They gave those at our table a laugh so fantastic!
Jake, your trouble in finding third floor
Will long be remembered by the wife you adore!

Now as this trip draws nigh to the end
I can honestly say—each of you is my friend
No longer strangers on the highway of life
We've grown much closer through our laughter and strife.

May God richly bless you we'd be overjoyed
To travel again with Gladys and Lloyd,
See you next trip, if the Lord will allow
That's all of my poem—So I'll sit down—right now!

Thoughts

Fall of Life

Trees whose colors come to life,
Whose limbs look dry and dead.
Flowers whose buds are tightly closed
To cold, bleak days ahead.
Grass whose blades once stood upright
But now lie trampled and bleached.
Birds whose songs once filled the air
Whose music can't now be reached.
Life, whose victims once were blind
To the mercilessness of fall,
Victims, whose happiness was found in spring,
Now resigned to answer their call.
Fate, whose beckoning finger points to soon,
Whose answer cannot be denied,
Winter, unwelcoming foe, at last
Casts a spell from which none can hide.
Life finally closes in like icy fingers of fall,
And one more victim answers that last call.

Unheeded Challenge

High above the mountain peak,
I see a cloud arise.
And through the lightning's pierced streak
It glows before my eyes.
The form is as a stormy sea
Raging white with foam,
The tiny spot thereon must be
A ship progressing home.
Then swift the tide of tossing waves
Sweeps o'er the gallant boat.
As fate announces watery graves,
No longer do they float.
Their cries alarm my spirit sore,
How can I heed their plea?
Then, as they're lost forevermore,
Their blood is cast on me.
How can I wash this stain so red?
My tortured soul cries loud.
Those I could have saved are dead.
Then vanishes my cloud.

Eternal Seasons

Bright the sun, as spring gives birth.
Pregnant is the fertile earth;
Full of life and promise to
Create a fine and splendid view.
Warm the sun in summer's sky.
Life so full; and hope so high.
Strong, and sure of what will be;
Armed to meet a destiny.
Sad the sun now kissing trees.
Time is come; So die the leaves.
One last breath before the blast
Suffocates, and fall is past.
Cold the sun of winter's morn.
All is dead that sun did borne.
Calm and still the earth will sleep
'Til nature calls out from the deep.
Then death shall cease once more to be
And life will beckon you and me.

Beyond a Garden Wall

Beyond a garden wall
Where moonbeams love to play,
Sweet peace guards o'er all
And nature has her way.

Their silence does not linger,
For near, a fountain flows,
Hark! Listen to a singer
As he flits among the rose.

The fragrance of the flowers
Floats on the balmy breeze,
The colors are like the rainbows
That stretch above the trees.

A mound that's newly made
Among the grass and flowers,
The print marks of a spade
Will disappear in hours.

Beyond a garden wall
This soul is at its rest,
Beneath this mound so small,
Nothing can molest;

His work on earth is over,
To his soul, peace is given,
Cares perplex him no more,
His life's reward is Heaven.

The Eyes of Heaven

Starry eyes of Heaven scan
In awe and admiration
Along the shores of every land,
The hills of every nation.

Valleys low, the rivers' flow.
Deserts bleak, the mountains' peak.
Prairies Wide, the ocean's tide.

Misty eyes of Heaven glow
With pride and adoration
Upon the world spread out below,
The art of God's creation.

Woodlands neat, the jungles' heat.
Tundra's cold, the tropics' mold.
Wastelands poor, the islands' moor.

Saddened eyes of Heaven gaze
O'er human population—
The dirt, the noise, the smoggy haze—
Thoughtless desecration.

Highways jammed, rivers dammed,
Building tall, playgrounds small.
People rushed, songbirds hushed.

Thoughtful eyes of Heaven fade
In fear and trepidation.
The careless world that man has made
Will breed annihilation.

Arise and Take Flight

Oh, troubled soul.
Spirit away above mountains of hate;
Rivers of greed,
Valleys of doubt.
Find thyself in the images of love,
Of gratitude
And well-being.
Climb to heights of confidence,
Sympathy
And understanding.
Flee from shame and exposure
And that self-degradation—pride.
Break the bonds of cynicism,
Chains of sarcasm and jealousy.
Escape the clutches of Fear;
The clammy fingers of Death.
Nourish thy being with kindness,
Humbleness
And perfection.
Drink from the fountains of faith.
Sip cool waters
Of generosity.
Saturate thy inner self with all
That which is God.
Oh, troubled soul,
Arise and take flight.

And So I

It's said that love can conquer all
The many harms that can befall
And so I love.

It's said that song can chase away
The darkest clouds of any day
And so I sing.

It's said that work can prevent ill
And shame the Caller to be still
And so I work.

It's said that smiles can win your foe
And dissipate his tales of woe
And so I smile.

But deep within I hear a voice
That tells me I will have no choice,
That nothing changes the Caller's mind,
And each must answer when it's time.
And so I die.

On Looking Down

What fascinating things we'd miss each day
If, as we hurriedly went our way.
We focus on objects at shoulder height;
By not looking down, we limit our sight.

Lessons on life are discerned at our feet,
Without which our Knowledge would be incomplete,
Meander awhile through the beauties that lie
Often unnoticed by those passing by.

Affirmation

Twigs are bent
And, snapped from life,
Are dying.
Leaves are blown
All around
They're lying.
But
Where they fell
The ground is dappled—
Veritably, May-appled.

Hope

From cold, brown earth,
Frosted in delicate
Green,
Tentatively emerge
Tender shoots
Drawn by the warmth
Of a spring day
Sun.
Tasting life,
Shoots burst forth
Into bloom,
Hope reigns!

Contrasts

Young and old,
Fragile, bold
Whole, broken
Quiet, spoken
Mighty, weak
Tenacious, meek
Alive, dying
Standing, lying
Straight and tall
Curved and small
Breakers, benders
Beginners, enders
Learned, untaught
Flexible, taut
Innocent, wise
Openness, guise

Contrast creates BEAUTY.

Protection

An ancient tree gives shelter to
A newly sprung, tender shoot,
Hovering so protectively
Until it can take root.

Time will claim the dying tree,
But near its falling place,
The younger, stronger one will be
Alive! I rest my case!

Condemnation

Who could have done such a damaging act?
Was it downed by machine or a handheld ax?
Did lightning strike this tree in its prime?
(That happens so often) but didn't this time.

Some little beavers were building a dam
To provide their families a home where they swam
Can, who cut trees to burn and to build,
Condemn these small critters who are so God-skilled?

It Was

A piece of equipment designed for much use,
A handsome tool any man might choose.
But time and weather, or maybe obtuseness,
Have over the years, rendered it useless.

Here it lies broken among the stones
Like a forgotten field of scattered bones,
Today, it's a doer that no longer does,
Yet evidence proves that it was, IT WAS!

Impression

Impressions here indicate
Some animal of late
Found a perfect place to rest.
A cozy, pleasant nest.

What impressions do we make
That neither time nor use can shake?
Will someone pause to ponder upon
Impressions we made before moving on?

Dark Beauty

Beauty is found mid ugliness
And truth among the lies,
Peace evolves from war and strife
And laughter among the cries.
Love sometimes resides near hate
And kindness lives with greed.
Joy reflects in spite of gloom
And flowers sprout with weed.
The best of life can be where you are,
If you want to feel "up," look down,
For often in the darkest place,
Beauty can be found.

Togetherness

Life emerges like a spring bouquet,
Up from the bowels of winter's decay,
Demanding sun and a chance to grow,
Responding to rain and winds that blow.

A single bloom could not survive
Without the help of those alive,
Who also need to replenish in kind,
Togetherness as predesigned.

Reflections on the Beatles

I like the words of the songs they write,
Put the beat is sometimes outta sight;
And, if you asked me, I really don't care
For some the outlandish apparel they wear;
But the effect of their music cannot be denied,
And oft when I hear it, I'm torn up inside,
And though of the younger set, they are the rage,
I get the message, in spite of my age.

Ramblings

He boasts with pride in song and shout
"It's swell to be a grandpa—"
Until the shocking truth comes out—
"I'm married to a grandma!"

I opened wide and showed the dentist
The tooth he should be taking,
And wouldn't you know, an hour ago
Another started aching!

Crying of a Guitar

Strums
Softly
Across
My memory,
Hums
Taunting
Melodies
Which vibrate
Images to life
In the caches of my heart.
I cry.

Sun Yellow

Vivid,
Shadow casting,
Yellow,
Reflecting
On my face.

Yellow flowers,
Smiling at me,
Yellow corn,
Nature's nourishment.

Yellow sky,
Singing brightly
To the receptive
Earth.
"Here am I!
See me!
I am sunshine."

A Sweeper

(I would read this poem to my students and ask what I was describing. They rarely were able to identify a sweeper.)

A long, skinny-necked
Hungry beastie
Buzzes angrily across
My carpet.
Devouring everything
In its path
Roaring loudly
When it bites off
More than it can
Swallow.

Squeaks

Silence, silence,
A tiny squeak
Speaks!
What is it
That comes to visit?
A mouse
In my house?
A swinging door?
A creaking floor?
Maybe it's a baby
Or a fraidy lady?

Sounds quite merry
Not scary.
I accept it
And I'll bet it
Keeps me
Awake!

Eating Watermelon

It's summertime and I am yellin'
For some good old watermelon,
Juicy, mushy, ripe, and sweet,
But very difficult to eat.
The juice is flowing down my chin,
Down both arms and up again,
I spit the seeds out—every one
And take a shower when I'm done.

Thoughts like Bees

Thoughts
Like bees swishing
Around in my mind
Flitting to and fro
Aimless
Pleasant—
Until gracefully
Landing
On a
Tender emotion
And I'm moved to
Action.

Emotion

Heating the blood,
Surging angrily
Through
Constricted
Passageways;
Clouding the vision
Like an opaque curtain
Drawn across
Once beautiful
Mind images.
Etching emotion
In razor-edged sensitivity,
Accelerating
Negative thoughts
To a maddening pace,
Heating the blood...
Jealousy? Frustration?
Rage? You Got It!

Silence

(We would read this during class and talk about silence when someone wants to talk and you don't want to listen.)

I hate to bother you
Silence.
But I'm hurting!
Silence.
I need to talk.
Silence.
Please listen.
Silence.
I need to know you hear.
Silence.
This awful feeling inside…
Silence.
Is suffocating me.
Silence.
Be there for me; be there!
Silence.
I'm not getting anywhere—
Silence.
Aren't we a destructive pair!
Silence.

Shades

Shade of darkness settle down
On sleepy countryside and town
And sweet surprise—
Are hidden from men's curious eyes.

Puffs of cloudlets hover low
To shelter from winds that blow
And tuck it in,
A weary world bogged down with sin.

Gentle breezes hum a song
That makes the night seem not so long
And with a tune
Reminds that night that dawn comes soon.

Velvet wings of sleep arise
To join the watch of murky skies
And so is blest,
A burdened race with needed rest.

Varied sounds caress the air
With strains that only night can share
And gives the earth
A sense of comfort and peace and worth.

Shades of dawning gently creep
Upon a world entranced in sleep
And with the light
Has gone the magic of the night.

To Be a Friend

To paint, to write, to make with hands
A beauty without end,
Is far less precious than the art
Of being just a friend.

The purple mounts, and lush green hills,
With azure skies do blend,
But never can a scene outshine
The beauty of a friend.

To conquer foes, to win the peace,
A broken world to mend,
Is not a greater task to dare
Than to be a loyal friend.

To create music, sweet and deep,
A mellow tone to rend,
Gives not the satisfaction as
The praises of a friend.

Though man might strive to win a goal,
And press, that fame attend,
No greater gift can God bestow
Than to learn to be a friend.

A Brilliant Mind

A brilliant mind is a gift beyond measure,
A key to the future, a rare, priceless treasure,
And he who possesses so great a prize
Is obliged to become, of all men, most wise,
For he holds the power to unlock the door
To answers, solutions, discoveries, and more.
He must find ways to improve man and earth,
For to him has been given, since the day of his birth,
The burden of bearing the weak and oppressed,
The ultimate duty of relieving earth's stress.
But brilliance cannot true brilliance impart
Unless God's presence lives deep in his heart.

The Real Man

Underneath the rush and hurry
Hidden deep beyond the worry
Swells a yearning for a chance to catch our breath.

Covered up by smiling faces
Unacknowledged in most cases
Lies a secret, anxious fear of pending death.

Shadowed oe'r by light of power
Cast aside in fortune's hour
There awaits the truth that life shall someday cease.

Buried deep beneath the pleasure
Guarded well by hoarded treasures
Breathes the hope that distant futures promise peace.

Barred within a wall of duties
Robbed by faking of its beauties
Burns the passion to be honest, kind, and true.

Shackled down by good intentions
Weighted down by self-pretensions
Lives a being that with nurture could be you.

Embers

A misty haze enshrines with care
The sacred hearth of Hope.
And glowing embers midst the ash
For life will ever grope.
So far removed from mortal mind
Or human thought or dream,
Almost attained by just a few
In shadow of Hope's beam.
And yet remote by hair's breadth width
As hope withdraws her glow
To test the strength and will of those
Who glimpse of promise show.
She leads ahead and just in view,
So near and yet so far,
And beckons with a hand of faith
To yonder brilliant star.
And well it is, that never reached
And always just beyond,
For goals of men will cease to be
If ever Hope is gone.
Life is given to us anew
By breath of living coals,
Restoring those who search for Death,
Reviving hopeless souls.

So, Cherish Hope and guard her well.
Your utmost dreams and fancies tell
Into her vibrant, listening ear.
Though out of reach, Hope will be near.

The Invisible Cycle

Rides the wind with restless force;
Victimizing the unattached.
Brags the wind in holing gales,
Intimidating, fierce, and proud.
Plays the wind with senseless puff,
Teasing and tugging at Nature's skirts.
Mourns the wind in painful groans—
Seeking attention and sympathy.
Croons the wind with lonely heart,
Whispering notes in pathetic tones.
Sings the wind to laughing trees,
Dancing on wings invisible and spright.
Dies the wind in breathless gasp
Dormant until nature awakens.

Sunbeams

One day when all was sunshine,
And clouds had gone to rest,
I lay and watch the sunbeams
Each trying to shine the best.

None could win, 'twas quite a race,
But how they brightened things,
For into the merry sunbeams,
Some songbirds flew to sing.

The birds influenced others,
To change their frames of mind,
For soon some little children
Were playing seek and find.

The children's merry laughter,
Has seemed to draw some kin,
For now I see parents
Acting young and gay again.

Let's take a hint from sunbeams,
And drive the clouds away,
Be merry even when it's dark
And all will soon be day.

If I Could Say

If I could say what I feel inside
I'd be a popular guy,
Instead of speaking, I run and hide,
I cannot tell you why
I cower behind a sycamore tree
And think of the nicest things,
But a strange numbness spreads over me
My words fly away on wings.
Such beautiful words, both good and kind
So desperately try to escape,
The noblest thoughts are locked in my mind,
I'm a dumb, inarticulate ape.
None of my friends shall ever hear
(Because I'm unable to say)
How great they are! How very dear
They are in every way,
But I can write, so write them I will—
These words I never have said,
"I love you, guys; You'll know just how much
The minute this poem is read."

Progress

PROGRESS, the breath of life
And doom of convention.
From the first moment of strife
To the last good intention.
Who dares to take a stand
Against so great a force
Is destined by his own hand
To it unrelenting course.
But rather, at the advent,
If the unknown and the new,
Give our unreserved consent;
Progress will see you through.

A Broader Walk

The walk that wraps around my house
Is narrow, made of stone,
And each who follows in its course
Must choose to walk alone.
Oh! One can always look ahead
Or often glance behind
To speak a word or cast a smile
To those likewise confined;
But I prefer a broader path,
Naught matters if it's wide,
For any path is shorter far
When walking side by side.
The narrow walk is made for those
Who choose to meditate
Upon the grossness of the world,
The outcome of its fate,
Or those whose burdens lay them low
And solitude is blessed,
Or those who weary of the noise
And seek a silent rest.
But I prefer a broader path,
In thought, in joy, in grief;
A clasp of hand, an echo step
Perpetuates belief.

What's the Good?

I work all day 'til setting sun
With many jobs still left undone.
I toss all night, too worn to sleep,
And rise each day to clean and sweep.
I go to work with lagging step
And hide the fact I have no pep.
I smile as though I feel just fine,
Of being tired, I give no sign,
And when the clock says time to go,
I hurry home—more work, you know!
"What's the good?" I often fret,
"The hurrieder I go, the behinder I get."
I have no time to catch my breath,
I seem to be working myself to death.
But still, when all is said and done,
I'll have to say, "It's sure been fun!"

A Little Seed

Ever in a chamber
Near the center of my heart
Lies a seed of good intention
That has never taken start.
Not that I've forgotten
Where the little seed is sown,
But I get somewhat discouraged
When I find it hasn't grown.
Dormant in its chamber,
Full of hope that soon will be
A chance for good intention
To walk hand in hand with me.

A Child's World

A world of dreams and fairy tales
Of pirate ships and monster whales.
A world of elves and magic wands,
Of boogie men and leprechauns.
A world of games and endless play,
Of hide and seek and races gay.
A world where fear is but a word
And pain and sickness are unheard.
A world where naught can ever harm
And death can never bring alarm.
A world where kindness rules supreme,
And nightmares are but silly dreams.
Oh, what a world that world would be,
But it's impossible, unfortunately,
For only in dreams is a child's world free
From the troubles that plague all Humanity.

Begin to Question

With carefree steps a child skips by,
No thoughts of questions—how or why,
No worries, perplexities, fears, nor dread,
No trepidation of what lies ahead.

An older lad with head cocked high,
Beholds the mystery of the sky,
And slight the stirring depths within
Awaken softly amid the din.

"I wonder where the world began;
I wonder who and how and when?"
And in his youth, the lad grows wise
By searching answers for the hows and whys.

He begins to question God and men,
Begins to search for what and when,
Believes in only the here and now,
Goes forth to answer why and how.

And in his quest for truths unknown,
His intellect has daily grown,
And in his grinding, ceaseless plan,
The untaught lad is now a man.

Out of the Page

By chance, while sorting through
A worn out pocketbook,
I came across a writing pad
And therein did I look.

A myriad of crooked lines
Boldly scanned the page,
And tiny, jagged doodle-dads
Sojourned in heated rage.

I smiled, for in my mind
I saw the childish hand
Which flitted fast and recklessly
To create art, unplanned.

A tear dropped to the busy page,
For time has claimed the child
Who wrote with gay abandonment
In manner free and wild.

He's since been taught to work
With careful thought and plan,
To plot a course and follow it—
To be a cautious man.

Picking Up Crumbs

He walked away.
I closed the door softly,
Smiling at the pleasantness
So unexpectedly come,
Now gone.
Returning to our empty cups,
I saw a chocolate crumb
Against a pristine placemat.
Reaching to remove
The misplaced morsel,
My hand hesitated,
Then dropped and paused.
In the rich brown crumbs
I see brown eyes glistening
Across our teacups,
Communicating thought and dreams,
Sharing lifelong plans and schemes.
If I brush the crumb aside,
Will memories of our visit
Glide into the corners of my mind,
And the pleasure of today be left behind?

Oh, for a Letter

Some people paint pictures
That crowds pause to praise,
Others make music
To brighten our days.
But I admire no one
A little bit better
Than those who can write
An interesting letter.
But oh, what a pity!
That those who *could* write
Have hidden their talent
From everyone's sight.
Of course there are reasons,
At least I've been told,
So I'll try not to argue,
Or heckle or scold.
"No news is good news—"
I cannot believe!
A short little note
Would bring such relief,
Especially for someone
Whom I will call Jim,
(It seems like forever
Since I've heard from him.)
"Now what could have happened?"
I cry in dismay,
To his beautiful wife
I will I will call Anna Kay.

I've heard that in Texas
Everything's better
So why couldn't they share it
In a cute little letter?
I'm getting so worried
I cry more and more,
When the mailman goes walking
Right past my front door.
If any who read this
Would just hear my plea
And tell my dear children
To please write to me—
I'd be ever so grateful
I know I'd feel better
If they would but write me
A long-looked-for letter.

Night Song

The night enfolds a weary, restless earth
And soothes it with a soft and smothered sigh,
The moonbeams dance aloft with joy and mirth
As songs of night birds sweetly float on high.
The dewdrops kiss the brown and withered grass,
And crickets croak aloud in peace and love,
The stillness creeps along on velvet paths,
While stars keep watch oe'r all from berths above.
The pools and lakes serenely settle down,
As playful winds of evening cease to blow.
The shades of darkness hide the ugly town,
Which takes on beauty in the mellow glow.

As night caresses, all the world is blest,
And every living creature finds its rest.

In the Prism of My Mind

In the prism of my mind
I often find
Glimmers of thought-seeds
Newly refined,
Unassigned
To actions which might
Assist in their flight
To fruition.
But lacking intuition,
I
Let them lie.
Eventually, to die—
Straining to achieve.
I now believe
I crush the very seed
That could amply
Feed
My deep-seated need.

I Can Almost See

I hear the sound of voices
Which seem to speak to me,
There's none I'd rather talk with
Than the mournful willow tree.

He whispers low his sorrows,
He hangs his head in shame,
And quietly I listen, 'til
Another calls my name.

I turn my head to westward,
And the sun begins his chat,
His warm rays tell me plainly
That he's happy where he's at.

Slowly bidding me adieu,
He sinks into the west,
Then twilight comes to visit
And the weary world's at rest.

The nightingale is singing
And its song delights my heart,
I can almost see her sitting
Where the hedges slightly part.

I can almost see the splendor,
I can almost see the night,
I can almost see the moon rise,
Almost, but not quite.

9/11

The world is broken, bleeding, in pain,
Never-forever to be the same,
Nations will ponder, discuss, unite,
Men and women will die as they fight

To avenge the attack of 9/11,
Nothing planned will be left undone
To bring to justice the deadly foe,
Who kill and destroy, wherever they go.

Will we succeed or will terror reign?
What can appease this horrific stain?
How can we conquer such deep-seated hate?
But conquer we must before it's too late.

So, drop the bombs, shoot powerful guns,
Fill those caves with stuff that stuns,
Flush the Taliban out of each cave,
Give retribution they seem to crave.

Capture every terrorist gang,
Try them by law and make them hang,
Attach the countries that give them aid,
Make sure all perpetrators have dearly paid.

Drive out terrorist from every land
But the fact remains, we understand,
As long as there's people still alive,
Hate and soullessness will somehow thrive.

Support Our Troops!

I don't want to hear your negative talk
About what's going on in the war,
Many have loved ones fighting there,
Give them support, I implore.

Our men and women in uniform
Don't need to hear all the "shouldn'ts,"
Most of such comments that speak of such
Are made by a bevy of "couldn'ts."

Support our troops with all of your heart,
Even though you may not agree
With the politics or the lack thereof—
Remember, we want to live free.

Pray for them daily, I urge of you,
That God will protect and guide them
Until this terrible war is finished,
Please, God, stay right there beside them.

Where's Freedom?

Has anyone seen freedom?
It seems she's run away,
She was standing here beside me,
Strong and proud and gay.

But then a bitter comment
Was spewn in bitter tone:
"Why don't we burn down buildings,
And statues made of stone?"

Another one agreeing, said,
"It's time to demonstrate.
Let's start a mass of violence
That will spread to every state."

Another said, "Yes, I agree.
We'll start in all the schools.
We'll show the one's in Congress
What we think of stupid rules."

I saw dear freedom waver
And her face grew still and wan
Her eyes blazed forth in fury—
Then quickly, she was gone.

Darkness settled heavily
On each one in that place
We sat not quite believing
There was sorrow on each face.

I cried, "We must find freedom,
And beg her to return.
Without her, we will perish!
When will we ever learn,

That freedom must be nourished
With love and sacrifice,
To enjoy freedom blessings
We must pay the highest price."

Has anyone seen freedom?
I've searched both night and day
I thought I heard her laugh once
Out where the children play

But when I asked the children
"Oh, help me if you can,"
They looked at me most quizzically,
And shook their heads and ran.

To a Three-Year-Old

Oh, how I yearn to hold you close
That naught would come to harm.
And how I long to shield and keep
You from danger and alarm.

I'd like to spread a loving wing
And hide you as a chick,
So, fear and pain were forced away,
And you felt not sorrow's prick.

But this, I know, would not be wise,
You must step out alone,
After all, you are now three;
How swiftly you have grown!

Would that I could keep you near
But then you'd never learn
That life is more than playing games
And that, pretty fires can burn.

I long to help you when you fall,
But help you, I cannot.
By falling, you can learn to stand,
So, conquer falls, my tot.

Becoming Forty

When you're young, you're strong and bold,
You never think about getting old,
You bounce with life and spread your wings,
Your spirit soars, your laughter rings.

Then, without warning, you've turned twenty,
Two decades gone, but still there's plenty
To offer you, so much satisfaction,
Along with trials and daily distraction.

The effervescence begins to fade,
You reap results of decisions made
In carefree years, in dream-filled days,
So unaware that in countless ways

The path you take when you are young
Affects the choices you now walk among—
Whether you're happy or discontented,
If you're at peace or by life tormented.

About the time you've adjusted to being thirty,
Life hands you a deal that's somewhat dirty,
You're hitting forty! A downhill trip!
Forty's a year you'd like to skip.

Remember, the best is still ahead;
(The only alternative is to be dead!)
Life for you is just beginning,
Each year that passes, proves you're winning!

Remember

Remember when you were in your teens?
You were full of energy, plans, and dreams,
Your world was filled with countless joys
Like buying clothes, ball games, and of course, boys.
Yes, there were times when your heart was broken
Over a misunderstanding or a harsh word spoken,

But just when you thought you had life figured out,
You turned around one day and, without a doubt,
Another decade had passed you by.
Now you are twenty, how times seems to fly!
In your twenties and married with a child or two!
Oh, what joys and responsibilities ensue!

Then life plays a trick that's downright dirty,
You look in the mirror and you've turned thirty,
Thirty and harried, overwhelmed and stressed
No time to worry about the way you're dressed.
No time for hobbies, just hubby and kids.
Your list of "to dos" outnumber the "dids."

When you were a teen, you were quick to speak
That anyone forty was ancient, antique?
Well, now you are forty and "over the hill,"
But you don't feel old, you plan and dream still,
The kids are going or gone by this time.
You've regained some energy you had in your prime,
You and your husband go places, do things,
Feeling the joy that togetherness brings.

Then around fifty there's an increase in relation
And you are quite ready for this next generation!
Grandbabies bring new joys like no other
Because you are now a special grandmother.
Your personal goals have been put aside
As you involve yourself in their lives with pride.

At sixty, it seems, the body turns sour,
Joints are so still, you've new aches every hour.
Oh, what a time of real disappointments!
Your "get up and go" has "got up and went,"
How sad to think of time and money you've spent.

When you turn seventy, time for reflections;
How does your life measure up to perfection?
Through all these years, God's been by your side
To encourage and bless you, to save you and guide,
Have you succeeded in doing His will?
In spite of your busyness, do you live for Him still?

Listen to me closely, each girl, each lady,
Someday it's possible you will all become eighty,
And now that I'm there, I can say for sure,
But when you are there, you've learned to endure,
To trust in the Lord in all that you do,
And to live day by day, knowing He'll take you through.

I happen to know of some ninety-year-olds
Who may read this today, how their history unfolds,
They've followed Jesus most of their lives,
And their Christian witness still shines and thrives.
No matter what age you happen to be
The question to ask is, "Has Jesus saved me?"

I happen to be one of the ninety-year-olds
And I love to remember how my history unfolds
I've followed Jesus since I was fourteen
And so many blessings from God have I seen.
No matter at what age He calls me to rest
I can honestly say that "My life has been blessed."

Life without Jesus is no life at all,
It's just passing time from birth to death's call,
And then it's too late to give God your heart,
He'll say, "I never knew you; Depart."
So right now, this moment, repent of your sin,
Ask Him to forgive you, and He will come in.

About the Author

Norma A. Hawkins at a very early age wanted to be a teacher, but it wasn't until she had been out of high school for eleven years that she began her college classes at the University of Illinois. She graduated with a BA in English in 1966 and began teaching at Westville Junior High. During the summers of the next few years, she attended the University of Illinois and earned her master's in education degree. While teaching at the junior high, she also taught several night classes at the Danville Area Community College.

In 1976, her principal nominated Norma to the Those Who Excel Program which recognizes outstanding teachers throughout the state of Illinois. Norma was one of eight finalist selected. She has had her teaching units, which included reading and writing poetry, to the State Gifted Department and by the *ASCD* journal, a publication for curriculum directors. Her biography appeared in the Outstanding Teachers of America index in 1972.

Throughout her career, she served as cooperating supervisor for student teachers from the University of Illinois and the Eastern

Illinois University. She has been a presenter at many county and state teacher workshop and conferences.

While teaching, she also sang with the gospel group called the Family of God Singers. They traveled on weekends, singing at churches and special events throughout the Midwest. Her love of poetry and music was her method of ministry. One of her original songs "Praise the Lord Anyhow" was published.

Norma now lives in an independent senior living facility. During the pandemic, she and the other tenants were isolated for thirteen months. During that time, the minister who came to preach at the Sunday Services was not allowed to come in. Norma felt that God was asking her to minister to those seniors, so she led worship services for thirteen months. She also played the piano for each service as a friend led the songs.

This ninety-year-old lady is asking the Lord to use this poetry book as another means of ministry and is praying that it will be an enjoyment and a blessing to the reader.

Mrs. Hawkins, a widow, has two sons, six grandchildren, and fourteen great-grandchildren.